ACROSS THE BORDER LINE

Exploring Big Themes from Colossians

Published by
Spring Harvest
14 Horsted Square
Uckfield
East Sussex TN22 1QL

First edition 1998

Acknowledgements
Scripture quotations taken from the HOLY BIBLE, NEW
INTERNATIONAL VERSION.
Copyright ©1973, 1978, 1984 by International Bible Society.
Used by permission of Hodder and Stoughton Limited.
All rights reserved.

"NIV" is a registered trade mark of International Bible
Society. UK trademark number 1448790

Printed and bound in Great Britain.

Spring Harvest. A Registered Charity.

ISBN   1 899788 20 4

SPRING HARVEST
Equipping the Church for action

ACROSS THE BORDER LINE

Exploring Big Themes from Colossians

compiled and edited by
Stephen Gaukroger and Peter Meadows

---

contributors

Jonathan Lamb	**Nick Mercer**	**Rob Parsons**	**Nick Pollard**
Salvation	False Teaching	Family	Evangelism
Richard Tiplady	**Rob Warner**	**Mark Greene**	**John Richardson**
World Mission	Spiritual Warfare	The World of Work	Pressing On

John Maile
Additional Biblical work in all sections

HOW TO GAIN THE MOST FROM THIS UNIQUE RESOURCE

This publication is a unique and valuable resource designed to help you learn and grow as a Christian. Use it to study by yourself, in a small group or in a larger seminar-style setting.

Rather than being designed as a book to be read, it is set out in ways that help you apply your Christian faith to some major issues.

Along with the commentary on Paul's letter to the church at Colossae there are —

❖ notes on some of the key issues raised in the letter,

❖ boxes and side pieces with facts, statistics and background,

❖ structured questions that take you to the heart of the issues.

The best way for you to use this material depends on the setting in which you study it. But whatever the setting, make sure you —

❖ have the notes in one hand and your Bible in the other.

❖ feel free to make notes and marks on the pages, perhaps using a highlighter to pick out the bits you like or want to go back to.

❖ look up the Bible verses as you go – using a range of translations to help bring out the meaning.

Remember, few people will choose to tackle every word written here. We all have different needs at different times. So here is a smorgasbord from which to select the topics and practical issues most relevant to you.

1. In a Seminar Format
These pages are a great basis for an eight week 'Alpha-style' series that blends up-front teaching with small group activities and personal application.

A detailed Leader's Guide is available to help you. It is based on the one used by the Spring Harvest speakers who first presented this material. The Guide —

❖ explains how the material can be taught creatively and relevantly.

❖ has additional questions to those printed in the margins of these pages.

❖ includes small group activities and interactive ideas.

The Leader's Guide is available from Spring Harvest. Call 01825 769000

2. In a Small Group
The content of this publication is also ideal for a series of Home Groups – for which the leader needs the Leader's Guide described above. Its contents includes teaching approaches and questions that have small groups in mind.

3. Personal Study
When working through these pages alone, tackle the content in bite-size chunks —

1 read and reflect on the relevant passage from Paul's letter to the Colossians

2 consider the notes explaining any of the additional information.

3 read the following section, which applies the issues that Paul raises to our own situation.

4 stop and think about the 'Question' sections in the margins.

5 use the 'fill in' activity at the end of each major section to help you identify what you have learnt and to reflect on it.

ACROSS THE BORDER LINE

Exploring big themes from Colossians

YOUR JOURNEY PLANNER

COLOSSIANS

1 Paul, an apostle of Christ Jesus by the will of God, and Timothy our brother,

[2]To the holy and faithful[1] brothers in Christ at Colosse:

Grace and peace to you from God our Father.[2]

Thanksgiving and Prayer

[3]We always thank God, the Father of our Lord Jesus Christ, when we pray for you, [4]because we have heard of your faith in Christ Jesus and of the love you have for all the saints—[5]the faith and love that spring from the hope that is stored up for you in heaven and that you have already heard about in the word of truth, the gospel [6]that has come to you. All over the world this gospel is bearing fruit and growing, just as it has been doing among you since the day you heard it and understood God's grace in all its truth. [7]You learned it from Epaphras, our dear fellow servant, who is a faithful minister of Christ on our[3] behalf, [8]and who also told us of your love in the Spirit.

QUESTION ?

What three things particularly strike you about the apostle Paul?

SETTING THE SCENE

Of all the churches to have received a letter from the Apostle Paul, the one at Colossae was certainly the least important. But the contents were vital.

1
2
3
4
5
6
7
8
9
10
11
12
13
14
15
16

This church was —

▶ A new church plant;
▶ In a multi-racial community;
▶ Beginning to find the religious views of those outside the church surface on the inside.

Against this background, they needed to be sure of what they believed – and relate it to their lives seven days a week.

The same message that Paul brought them rings true for you today. Jesus is supreme in every situation and for every circumstance.

The city

Colossae was on a bank of the river Lycus in what is now Turkey:

▶ about 100 miles from the great city of Ephesus;
▶ in a fertile valley which produced large crops of figs and olives;

BACKGROUND

PAUL – THIS IS YOUR LIFE:

Paul could have had no idea what impact his writings would have on the lives of millions.

1. He was born at the same time as Jesus. And most of his 'apostle' work was AD36-60.

2. His death was probably Rome AD62-64 – most likely as a martyr.

3. He was a committed Pharisee – which would have meant —

   ❖ he believed in one God, and the coming of the new age,

   ❖ he believed in the resurrection of the body at the end time for judgement,

   ❖ he observed tradition above and beyond the law, being extremely zealous and committed to his faith,

   ❖ he persecuted Christians because of his zeal, not because of being a Pharisee.

4. His encounter with the risen Christ was in AD33, either on the road to Damascus (Acts 9:3–6) or in Damascus (Gal 1:15–17). He considered this equal to a resurrection appearance and therefore counted himself as an apostle.

5. His task was an apostle to the Gentiles.

6. He was an educated, well-read man, moving in and out of the Graeco-Roman world, and his main language was Greek.

7. His trade was tent-making (Acts 18:3), which he seemed to combine with his new-found calling.

8. His writings, though sent to specific places for specific purposes, are the earliest New Testament writings that we have. They trace an emerging church and the developing theology of these first Christians.

9. He may have been of small stature and not a man for public speaking. But he appears to be a debater in small groups – taken from his Jewish background.

10. We can assume he did not marry, and that he carried some continuing affliction with him throughout his ministry.

1 ▶ on the main road from Ephesus to the river
2 Euphrates.
3
4 Four hundred years earlier, it had been a great city –
5 large, wealthy and populous. But by the time of Paul it
6 had declined to being only a small town, overshadowed
7 by Laodicea and Hierapolis, both half a day's walk away.
8
9 Its chief commercial significance lay in its wool
10 industry. And the area was notorious for earthquakes
11 which, on occasion, almost certainly afflicted Colossae.
12

13 The church

14 The Christian community in Colossae was one of
15 several in the area that had resulted from outreach by
16 the church founded in Ephesus, as recorded in Acts 19
17 (*c* AD52–55).
18

19 Colossae was found by Epaphras, himself a native
20 Colossian and probably converted under Paul's ministry
21 in Ephesus (cf. 1:7; 4:12–13).
22

23 It would seem that most of the church were Gentiles
24 (cf. 1:21,27; 2:13).
25

26 The evidence for this is that —
27 ▶ Paul speaks of them as 'outsiders' who have been
28 brought 'inside';
29 ▶ there are very few Old Testament allusions;
30 ▶ 3:5–7 seems to refer to specifically Gentile vices;
31 ▶ almost nothing is said about the need for Jewish
32 and Gentile Christians to be reconciled to each
33 other.
34

35 The writer

36 There is no good reason to doubt that **Paul** wrote the
37 letter – almost certainly from Rome during his first
38 term of imprisonment.
39

40 OVERVIEW OF COLOSSIANS CHAPTER 1

41 The letter opens in the way that letters did at that time
42 – naming the author, briefly describing the recipients
43 and adding a short greeting in the form of a
44 prayer-blessing.
45

46 Paul then gives thanks for the Colossians (vv.3–5),
47 particularly for three great hallmarks of real Christianity

---

EPAPHRAS

Epaphras was a native of Colossae, a preacher and a companion of Paul. His name is derived from the word for charming. He was an evangelist who had worked in Laodicea and Hieropolis as well as in Colossae.

9For this reason, since the day we heard about you, we have not stopped praying for you and asking God to fill you with the knowledge of his will through all spiritual wisdom and understanding. 10And we pray this in order that you may live a life worthy of the Lord and may please him in every way: bearing fruit in every good work, growing in the knowledge of God, 11being strengthened with all power according to his glorious might so that you may have great endurance and patience, and joyfully 12giving thanks to the Father, who has qualified you[4] to share in the inheritance of the saints in the kingdom of light. 13For he has rescued us from the dominion of darkness and brought us into the kingdom of the Son he loves, 14in whom we have redemption,[5] the forgiveness of sins.

QUESTION ?

What three things particularly strike you about the church in Colossae?

---

1 2 Or *believing*
2 2 Some manuscripts *Father and the Lord Jesus Christ*

that they were showing —

- Faith in Jesus
- Spirit-inspired love for fellow-Christians (cf v.8);
- Hope, with its twin aspects of —

    a present reality – it is even now ready for us in heaven

    a confident expectation for the future – it is stored up for us until we enter into it.

Paul points to the **gospel**, as shared with them by Epaphras, as having produced their life-changing experience. This gospel is —

- **reliable** – "the word of truth" (v.5)
- **universal** – "all over the world" (v.6)
- **effective** – "is bearing fruit and growing" (v.6)
- **an expression of God's grace** (v.6).

Having started so well, they need to progress in their faith. Paul constantly prays for them to receive (vv.12-13, 21-22) —

- wisdom and understanding – to know what God wants and so live a daily life that pleases him through good works and a deepening relationship with him;
- strength – to keep going;
- a joyful realisation – of the amazing transformation that God has accomplished in them through the death of Jesus.

Then, using what may be an early Christian statement of faith – which would have been familiar to the Colossians – Paul celebrates the unique supremacy of Jesus (vv.15–20) —

- in creation (vv.15–17)
- in the church (v.18)
- in the new creation (vv.19–20).

Jesus is the hub of salvation, the head of the church and the heart of redemption.

This is the essence of the gospel of which Paul is a minister. A ministry —

- expressed in suffering servanthood (vv.24–25,29);
- centred on the now open secret of God's love for Gentiles as well as Jews (vv.25–27);
- with the goal of presenting everyone perfect in Christ (v.28).

QUESTION ?

In what ways is the gospel having this effect in your life and in your church?

The Supremacy of Christ

[15]He is the image of the invisible God, the firstborn over all creation. [16]For by him all things were created: things in heaven and on earth, visible and invisible, whether thrones or powers or rulers or authorities; all things were created by him and for him. [17]He is before all things, and in him all things hold together. [18]And he is the head of the body, the church; he is the beginning and the firstborn from among the dead, so that in everything he might have the supremacy.

[3] 7 Some manuscripts *your*

[4] 12 Some manuscripts *us*

[5] 14 A few late manuscripts *redemption through his blood*

GOSPEL

The Greek word used in the New Testament and translated as 'joyful tidings' and 'good news' has an Old Testament background. In Isaiah 40–46 it is used to describe the declaration of Jerusalem's deliverance from bondage. In Isaiah 61:1–2 it is used to describe a wider announcement of liberation for the oppressed.

This last passage became the text of Jesus' first preaching at Nazareth, where he gave notice that it had been fulfilled as he spoke (Luke 4:17–21).

Jesus' message was described as the gospel of the kingdom of God. Its contents are set out in his parables, where the father's loving mercy and free forgiveness – shown to those who were undeserving and the outcasts – is presented with vividness and warmth.

With Jesus' death and resurrection a new phase of 'the gospel' begins. The one who was the preacher now becomes the content of the preaching. His followers – commissioned to preach the gospel after his departure – proclaimed him as the one in whom the father's pardoning grace had drawn near.

The basic elements in the gospel message were —

1. The prophecies have been fulfilled and the new age inaugurated by the coming of Christ.

2. He was born into the family of David.

3. He died according to the Scriptures, to deliver his people from this evil age.

4. He was buried and raised again the third day, according to the Scriptures.

5. He is exalted at God's right hand as Son of God, Lord of living and dead.

6. He will come again to judge the world and consummate his saving work.

For the first generation after Christ's ascension, the gospel was exclusively a spoken message. The earliest written record of the gospel appeared in the 60s.

Adapted from 'New Dictionary of Theology' (IVP)

1
2
3
4
5
6
7
8
9
10
11
12
13
14
15
16
17
18
19
20
21
22
23
24
25
26
27
28
29
30
31
32
33
34
35
36
37
38
39
40
41
42
43
44
45
46
47

SALVATION
– PASSPORT CONTROL

Can we ever understand the extent of our own need, the depth of God's love – and the significance of all that Jesus did to rescue us?

COLOSSIANS 1:19–20

Paul first sets out the supremacy of Christ in both creation and the church (vv.15–18). Then he climaxes this section by adding two further aspects of this supremacy.

The first aspect of Christ's supremacy is that he perfectly shows us what God is like.

Using ideas from the Old Testament (v.19), Paul says that God has freely chosen – literally 'delighted' – to be uniquely and permanently (cf 2:9) present – literally to take up residence – in all his fullness in Christ.

This means that all that is true about God in respect of what he is like and what he does is perfectly displayed and demonstrated in Christ. In him we see God, hear God and meet God.

The second aspect of Christ's supremacy is that he is the unique agent of a universal reconciliation (v.20) – a reunion and restoration achieved through his death on the cross.

By *reconciliation*, Paul means that —
- In Christ's death his lordship over the universe has been restored;
- Heaven and earth have been brought back into their divinely ordained order under the headship of Christ. And the day is coming when, willingly or unwillingly, all things will acknowledge that lordship.

This does not mean that everyone is automatically 'saved'. The whole creation – including the spiritual powers – was created in, through and for Christ. But —
- the powers have rebelled;
- the created order has been disrupted by sin;
- chaos and disorder have appeared.

The word *salvation* is one of the great jargon words of the Christian faith – often used but much less understood. The way it is most used in 'real life' is in terms of 'preservation from loss or calamity'. Goal-scorers become the *salvation* of their team. Zit cream can be *salvation* for a teenager.

[19]For God was pleased to have all his fullness dwell in him, [20]and through him to reconcile to himself all things, whether things on earth or things in heaven, by making peace through his blood, shed on the cross.

[21]Once you were alienated from God and were enemies in your minds because of[6] your evil behaviour. [22]But now he has reconciled you by Christ's physical body through death to present you holy in his sight, without blemish and free from accusation—[23]if you continue in your faith, established and firm, not moved from the hope held out in the gospel. This is the gospel that you heard and that has been proclaimed to every creature under heaven, and of which I, Paul, have become a servant.

Paul's Labour for the Church

[24]Now I rejoice in what was suffered for you, and I fill up in my flesh what is still lacking in regard to Christ's afflictions, for the sake of his body, which is the church. [25]I have become its servant by the commission God gave me to present to you the word of God in its fullness—[26]the mystery that has been kept hidden for ages and generations, but is now disclosed to the saints.

[6] 21 Or *minds, as shown by*

16

None of this captures the fullness behind the concept of salvation as expressed in the Bible – and defined in the dictionary as "saving of the soul from sin and its consequences".

The word *salvation* is often used in the Old Testament to describe the many acts of God in saving his people. But in the New Testament it is focused in Jesus, whose name means '*Yahweh is salvation*' (Matt 1:21). The Christian teaching about salvation hinges around a unique emphasis on Christ and his cross.

To fully understand the concept of *salvation* it is necessary to explore a cluster of central themes in the Christian message. These range through —
- the nature of human rebellion, which provokes the need for salvation;
- the severity of God's wrath and judgement, from which we need to be rescued;
- the human-divine nature of Jesus Christ the Saviour;
- the way in which we are saved through the sacrificial death of Jesus;
- the universal dimensions of the salvation that Jesus has secured.

Paul is clear when writing to the Colossians about the reality of salvation. However, he addresses the theme far more fully in his letter to the Christians in Rome.

In two major passages (Rom 3:19–26 and 5: 6–11) he encapsulates the broad themes that underlie a biblical understanding of salvation.

OUR HUMAN CONDITION

Salvation is God's response to human sinfulness – which Paul describes in Romans 6 in a series of graphic terms.

He says we are —
Powerless (v.6)
We are not able to save ourselves or to reach God's reasonable expectations. We are not able to —
- undo the past;
- overcome sin's hold upon us;
- deal with its consequences of guilt, death and judgement.

1
2
3
4
5
6
7
8
9
10
11
12
13
14
15
16
17
18
19
20
21
22
23
24
25
26
27
28
29
30
31
32
33
34
35
36
37
38
39
40
41
42
43
44
45
46
47

ROMANS 3:19–26, 5:6–11

3 ¹⁹Now we know that whatever the law says, it says to those who are under the law, so that every mouth may be silenced,and the whole world held accountable to God. ²⁰therefore no-one will be declared righteous in his sight by observing the law; rather through the law we become concious of sin.

²¹But now a rightousness from God, apart from law, has been made known, to which the Law and the Prophets testify. ²²This righteousness from God comes through faith in Jesus Christ to all who believe. There is no difference, ²³for all have sinned and fall short of the glory of God, ²⁴and are justified freely by his grace through the redemption that came through Christ Jesus. ²⁵God presented him as a sacrifice of atonement, through faith in his blood. He did this to demonstrate his justice, because in his forbearance he had left the sins committed beforehand unpunished ²⁶—he did it to demonstrate his justice at the present time, so as to be just and the one who justifies those who have faith in Jesus.

5 ⁶You see, at just the right time, when we were still powerless, Christ died for the ungodly. ⁷Very rarely will anyone die for a righteous man, though for a good man someone might possibly dare to die. ⁸But God demonstrates his love for us in this: While we were still sinners, Christ died for us.

⁹Since we have now been justified by his blood, how much more shall we be saved from God's wrath through him! ¹⁰For if, when we were God's enemies, we were reconciled to him through the death of his Son, how much more, having been reconciled, shall we be saved through his life! ¹¹Not only is this so, but we also rejoice in God through our Lord Jesus Christ, through whom we have now received reconciliation.

PRESSING ON

EVANGELISM
FALSE TEACHING
SALVATION
UNLIMITED ENTRY·UNLIMITED
UNLIMITED ENTRY·UNLIMIT

"Fear God, yes, but don't be afraid of him." **J.A.Spender**

1 **Ungodly (v.6)**
2 We are out of harmony —
3 ▶ with God;
4 ▶ with others;
5 ▶ with ourselves.
6
7 **Sinners (v.8)**
8 We have declared our independence, turned away from
9 God's ways and fallen short of his standards.
10
11 **Enemies (v.10)**
12 We are actively hostile towards God, and in rebellion
13 towards him.
14
15 Paul is very deliberate in emphasising that all people are
16 in this state. Human sin and rebellion are a **universal**
17 condition.
18

QUESTION ?

Where do you see evidence of this–
▶ in society at large?
▶ in others?
▶ in your own life?

BACKGROUND

THE FALL

The cast

A man, a woman, a snake and a piece of fruit – together they convey the fall of creation in a graphic and memorable way. And it is the meaning of Genesis, not the detail, that matters.

The beginning

The backdrop was a place of harmony, peace, and order – most importantly between the creation and the creator. "It's good", God said.

The crash

The 'why' of it all is beyond our understanding. But God treated Adam and Eve as morally responsible and accountable creatures.

God had spoken his desire, his Word, and he wished to see his creatures' response. The reverse would have left our relationship with our creator a forced, involuntary, abstract reaction.

The forbidden choice was the material and aesthetic psychological amd mental enrichment over the spiritual lifeline —

❖ Eve listened to the created rather than the creator.

❖ She chose to see God's word as subject to her own judgement.

The serpent's interpretation was that through choosing against God you would find the truth and be like gods. The ultimate gain would be power, and God would be a rival.

Kicked out

The lie was told – and they fell for it. And through it all of creation fell short of being 'good'.

Their citizenship of the kingdom had been forfeited.

The way back

"Take and eat" were the words of temptation.

"Take and eat" was the invitation to the disciples of Jesus – to remember his death that was the key to the new kingdom. Not the deceiver, but the liberator.

In Romans 3:9–23 he underlines that no-one is righteous; all have sinned; and therefore everyone – without exception – must face God's just anger.

GOD'S SENTENCE

In his letter to the Romans, Paul explains that, because God is fair and just, he demands a sentence against us that is fair and just. This is why —

▶ God cannot ignore the extent and consequences of human rebellion.

▶ God's wrath "is being revealed from heaven against all the godlessness and wickedness of men" (1.18).

▶ The verdict against us is that we deserve judgement. "Because of your stubbornness and your unrepentant heart, you are storing up wrath against yourself for the day of God's wrath, when his righteous

judgement will be revealed" (2:5).

This righteous judgement of God includes death – physical and spiritual.

It is not that God is vengeful, or setting unreasonable standards. Rather, it is that sin and absolute purity do not mix – like oil and water. The contamination of sin has no place in the perfect environment of God's presence.

SALVATION NOW AND THEN

When the Bible speaks about salvation, it does so in language that suggests

- past – "those who *have been* saved" (Eph 2:5, 8).
- present – "those who are *being* saved" (1 Cor 1:18; 2 Cor 2:15);
- future – "He [Jesus] will appear … to bring salvation to whose who are waiting for him." (Heb 9:28). See also Acts 2:21; Rom 13:1; 1 Cor 5:5; 1 Pet 1:15.

While Paul links our salvation to the moment of our regeneration, he frequently hints at its eternal dimensions. For example: "But when the kindness and love of God our Saviour appeared, he *saved* (present) us, not because of righteous things we had done, but because of his mercy. He *saved* (present) us through the washing of rebirth and renewal by the Holy Spirit, whom he poured out on us generously through Jesus Christ our Saviour, so that, having been justified by his grace, we *might become* (future) heirs having the *hope* (future) of eternal life" (Titus 3:4–7).

Our salvation is a present reality and a future expectation of which we can be certain.

GOD'S INITIATIVE

The New Testament constantly makes it clear that salvation is all to do with what God has done, and not what we do.

The story of the Bible is the story of the fulfilment of God's everlasting purpose.

- It was God's plan from the beginning to restore us and his whole creation back to what we were intended to be.

Line numbers (right margin): 1–47

QUESTION ?

How do you view your own salvation in terms of–

- the past?
- the present?
- the future?

"He is no fool who gives what he cannot keep to gain what he cannot lose." **Jim Elliot**

HOPE

When the New Testament speaks of hope, it means something much more than 'being hopeful'. Rather, the emphasis is on something of which we can be sure and certain.

To 'hope' means to look forward expectantly for God's future activity. Our confidence is based on God's past activity in Jesus Christ, who points the way to God's purposes for his creation.

The Christian lives in hope and expectancy rather than in the fullness of the kingdom, walking in confident faith rather than by what can be seen (2 Cor 5:7).

1 ▶ Central to God's initiative is what Jesus did
2 through his death on the cross.
3
4 The Bible uses several strong images and illustrations to
5 help us understand 'the mystery' of the cross.
6
7 **The cross – a demonstration of love**
8 "God demonstrates his own love for us in this: while we
9 were still sinners, Christ died for us" (Rom 5:8).
10
11 The central theme of God's work of salvation is his love
12 and undeserved favour towards us.
13
14 This means that the cross is not simply a wonderful
15 example of self-sacrifice. Jesus' death was a
16 demonstration of God's love *related to our need* – as the
17 quote in the margin on the next page helps make clear.
18
19 The love of God is seen in all its fullness at the cross
20 because it was there that Christ suffered for our sins –
21 "the just for the unjust, that he might bring us to God"
22 (1 Peter 3:18, AV. See also 1 Peter 2:24; 2 Cor 5:21).
23
24 Augustine once called the cross the pulpit from which
25 Christ preached God's love to the world. While Martin
26 Luther said that to understand the Christian message it
27 was necessary to start with the wounds of Christ.
28

29 **The cross – seen in the language of the law court**
30 Paul uses legal language – and the word *justified* – in
31 Romans 3 and 5 to describe our situation and the
32 initiative that God took in Jesus.
33
34 He says we are —
35 ▶ "justified freely" (3:24);
36 ▶ "justified through faith" (5:1);
37 ▶ "justified by his blood" (5:9).
38
39 In this way, Paul presents —
40 ▶ God as the Judge and ourselves as the accused –
41 guilty and deserving judgement.
42 ▶ Christ's death as the penalty that has been paid so
43 that we can be pronounced forgiven.
44 ▶ The judge effectively stepping out from his seat,
45 having passed sentence, and taking the
46 punishment himself.
47

"The salvation of a single soul is more important than the production or preservation of all the epics and tragedies in the world."
C.S. Lewis

QUESTION ?

In what ways is Jesus' death different from the death of a martyr dying for a cause?

JUSTIFICATION

Justification is essentially a concept from the world of the legal system – yet it entails more in spiritual terms. It is a declaration of both innocence and righteousness.

Christ's death for our sins provides the basis on which God can justly declare the believer to be righteous (3:21–4:25). Paul makes it very clear that we are justified by faith (5:1), not by our actions.

God not only declares the believer to be righteous; God infuses new spiritual life – a righteousness actually *experienced* through faith in Jesus Christ (Gal 3:21–26).

Adapted from *The Applied Bible Dictionary*, Kingsway

The cross – seen in the language of sacrifice

"God presented him as a sacrifice of atonement" (3:25).

Here Paul uses the Jewish temple rituals to illustrate what the death of Jesus achieved.

- In the temple.
- Sacrifices were made to turn away God's wrath against the sinner.
- An animal became the substitute for the sinner – dying in their place.

In the same way, Jesus took our place through his death on the cross. Indeed, these activities in the Old Testament were a picture of what would happen through Jesus and his death.

Paul explains that it is as though someone who was totally blameless took the punishment in the place of someone who was guilty.

The wrath and judgement of God – which we deserved – have been borne by Jesus' sacrificial death.

The cross – seen in the language of freedom

"We are justified freely by his grace through the redemption that came by Christ Jesus" (3:24).

The word *redemption* is one that Paul borrowed from the commercial market place.

- If a slave was purchased and then set free, they were said to be *redeemed*.
- A prisoner of war could be *ransomed* or *redeemed* by his family if an appropriate price were to be paid.

Jesus was the first to use this picture. He described his mission as coming "to give his life as a ransom for many" (Mark 10:45). His death was to pay the price for our freedom.

Paul also picks up this theme when he says, "You are not your own. You are bought with a price" (1 Cor 6:19,20). See also 1 Peter 1:18–20.

The cross – in the language of human relationships

We were God's enemies, Paul said – so serious is the

"If I were sitting at the end of a pier and someone jumped into the water and got drowned 'to prove his love for me', I should find it quite unintelligible.
I might be much in need of love, but an act in no rational relation to any of my needs could not prove it.
But if I had fallen over the pier and were drowning, and someone sprang into the water and, at the cost of making my fate his own, saved me from death, then I should say, 'Greater love hath no man than this'.
I should say it intelligibly because there would be an intelligible relation between the sacrifice which love made and the necessity from which it redeemed."
James Denny

REDEMPTION

A word deriving its meaning from the slave market – 'To be bought with a price.' Just as God 'purchased' his people out of slavery in Egypt, so now he has paid the price, in his son, to set free the sin-slaves in every generation.

RECONCILIATION

This is the bringing together of two parties who are in a state of hostility or estrangement from one another. Only a being who was fully God (1:19) could bring about a reconciliation between two such opposites – a holy God and a rebellious, fallen world.

1 effect of our rebellion. But God's saving purpose is to
2 bring about *reconciliation.*
3
4 "For if, when we were God's enemies, we were
5 reconciled to him through the death of his Son, how
6 much more, having been reconciled, shall we be saved
7 through his life!" (Romans 5:10).
8
9 Christ's death makes us no longer enemies of God, but
10 his friends; Christ's death brings us back home, where
11 we belong. We are citizens of the Kingdom of the Son
12 (Col 1:13). The hostility between us is over.
13
14 We are —
15 ◗ no longer alienated but reconciled;
16 ◗ no longer enemies but children.
17
18 It is as though one person could take the punishment
19 for all the injustice that has created hostility in
20 Ireland –
21 ◗ restoring perfect peace to the community.
22 ◗ making it possible for all who have done wrong
23   to be at peace with each other.
24
25 Reconciliation, as conveyed in the New Testament,
26 covers the further idea of 'peace'. Christ's death means
27 the end of hostilities and the beginning of peace on a
28 cosmic scale.
29
30 Christ's work of reconciliation was "to reconcile to
31 himself all things, making peace by the blood of his
32 cross" (Col 1:20).
33
34 Just as the whole of creation felt the impact of the
35 rebellion that took place in the Garden of Eden, so it
36 will receive the benefit of Christ's sacrifice on the cross.
37
38 **The cross – in the language of victory**
39 To human eyes, the death of Jesus – on the cross, as a
40 criminal – oozed failure. But Paul paints a very different
41 picture. It is one where, through his death, Jesus —
42 ◗ defeated the opposition
43 ◗ took away their weapons so that the battle was
44   over for ever.
45
46 The death of Jesus was a place of glory in the midst of
47 apparent shame. A victory in apparent defeat.

"The Judge has pronounced us righteous, the Father has welcomed us home."
Rev Dr John Stott

QUESTION ?

What are some of the differences that Christ's death has made?

QUESTION?

In what ways did Jesus 'win' through his death on the cross?

Paul tells the Colossians that Jesus not only forgave us all our sins, but (Col 2:14,15) —

▶ "having cancelled the written code, with its regulations, that was against us and stood opposed to us, he (Jesus) took it away, nailing it to the cross.

▶ "Having disarmed the authorities, he (Jesus) made a public spectacle of them, triumphing over them by the cross".

John, in his Gospel, also highlights the same paradox. He records that —

▶ Jesus said his death would be the time for the Son of Man to be glorified (John 12:23, 27).

▶ Jesus said, "Now is the time for judgement on this world; now the prince of this world will be driven out" (John 12:31).

The work of salvation includes victory over Satan.

▶ "The reason the Son of God appeared was to destroy the devil's work" (1 John 3:8).

▶ "That by his death, he (Jesus) might destroy him who holds the power of death – that is, the devil" (Heb 2:14).

OUR RESPONSE

Paul has described —

▶ our human condition;

▶ God's just sentence;

▶ God's loving initiative towards us.

Paul also highlights the response of faith that people must make if God's saving purposes are to include them personally.

The impact of the death of Jesus depends on our response. The offer of forgiveness and a new citizenship has to be accepted – in the same way that an asylum seeker has to accept the offer of safety and the right to stay.

It is through our faith and reliance on what was achieved on the cross that salvation becomes ours.

As Paul wrote —

▶ "A man is justified by faith" (Rom 3:28).

▶ "This righteousness from God comes through

QUESTION?

List –

▶ what Jesus did to make our salvation possible.

▶ what we must do to receive the benefit.

"To know Christ is not to speculate about the mode of his incarnation, but to know his saving benefits." **Philip Melanchton**

"Don't matter how much money you got, there's only two kinds of people: there's saved people and there's lost people." **Bob Dylan**

1
2
3
4
5
6
7
8
9
10
11
12
13
14
15
16
17
18
19
20
21
22
23
24
25
26
27
28
29
30
31
32
33
34
35
36
37
38
39
40
41
42
43
44
45
46
47

1   faith in Jesus Christ to all who believe"
2   (Rom 3:22) .
3   ▶ Forgiveness comes "through faith in his blood"
4   (Rom 3:25).
5   ▶ God "justifies those who have faith in Jesus"
6   (Rom 3:26).
7
8 Our response is to *repent* and believe on Jesus.
9
10 A common mistake, during the history of the church,
11 has been for people to think that salvation must be
12 earned through religious duties or acts of goodness. But
13 Jesus came to free us from the bondage of duty and
14 ritual. We are destined for heaven, not because of what
15 we have done but because of what Jesus has done.
16
17 To repent is to take a radical new direction. Jesus
18 started his ministry by preaching, "Repent and believe
19 the good news" (Mark 1:15).
20
21 Peter, preaching in Athens, emphasises that repentance
22 is a universal command from God: "In the past, God
23 overlooked such ignorance, but now he commands all
24 people everywhere to repent" (Acts 17:30).
25

> "Modern man's loss of a sense of being sinful doesn't spring from a feeling that he is inherently good. Rather, it springs from his feeling of being inherently ineffectual."
> **Brendan Francis**

Repentance opens the way for faith, as happened at Pentecost when Peter told the people to "Repent and be baptised" (Acts 2:38).

PASSPORT

Citizen of Heaven
The Kingdom of God's Son

Name of holder:_____

Date of issue (if known): _____

Previous citizenship: _____

Reason for travel: _____

Distinguishing marks: _____

_____

Next of kin:_____

Expiry date:_____

Signature of holder: _____

QUESTION ?

Those who have experienced salvation were once 'aliens' (Col 1:21) but are now citizens of 'The Kingdom of the Son' (Col 1:13,14).
As a citizen of this kingdom, how would your passport read?

WORLD MISSION
– THE FAR COUNTRY

The good news about Jesus is for the whole world. Every nation, tongue and tribe. But there is still much to do.

COLOSSIANS 1:27–29

Paul writes about the work God has given him (1:24–2:5). The heart of this task is making known a 'mystery'.

This mystery, he says, is —
- a divine secret which had been hidden until the coming of Christ;
- now an open secret;
- that God's love embraces Gentiles as well as Jews – and that, in Christ, Gentiles and Jews are now included in the one people of God.

This meant that God's love was for all people everywhere.

Four particular things are true about this mystery (v.27).

It is magnificent – God shares with the *Gentiles* the 'glorious riches' of salvation (cf especially Eph 1:7,18; 2:4,7; 3:8,16). In fact he shares nothing less than the glory of God himself (cf 2 Cor 3:18).

It is universal – It is 'among the Gentiles' that the mystery has been made known. Those who were 'outsiders' are now to be found 'in Christ' (cf Eph 2:11–22).

It is Christ-centred – 'Christ in you' or, equally true, 'Christ among you' as in the plural. The first emphasises Christ living in each Gentile believer through their personal experience of him. The second emphasises the presence of Jesus among and within the Christian community (cf v.24).

It is forward-looking – 'the hope of glory'. Being included among the people of God in Christ now gives the assurance of sharing the full glory of the life to come.

Paul continues by emphasising that there is more to do than simply 'making known' the good news about Jesus (v.28). His mission – and ours – was not only to 'proclaim him'. It also involved —
- "Counselling and teaching everyone with all

GENTILES

A non-Jewish individual or people group. Little hostility is shown towards Gentiles in the Old Testament; indeed there are some promises of blessing (e.g., Isaiah 45:22). There is much greater tension in the New Testament period when non-Jews were viewed negatively spiritual (cf Eph 2:12) and treated suspiciously when they turned to Christ. (See early chapters of Acts.)

[27]To them God has chosen to make known among the Gentiles the glorious riches of this mystery, which is Christ in you, the hope of glory.

[28]We proclaim him, admonishing and teaching everyone with all wisdom, so that we may present everyone perfect in Christ. [29]To this end I labour, struggling with all his energy, which so powerfully works in me.

2 I want you to know how much I am struggling for you and for those at Laodicea, and for all who have not met me personally. ²My purpose is that they may be encouraged in heart and united in love, so that they may have the full riches of complete understanding, in order that they may know the mystery of God, namely, Christ, ³in whom are hidden all the treasures of wisdom and knowledge. ⁴I tell you this so that no one may deceive you by fine-sounding arguments. ⁵For though I am absent from you in body, I am present with you in spirit and delight to see how orderly you are and how firm your faith in Christ is.

Freedom From Human Regulations Through Life With Christ

⁶So then, just as you received Christ Jesus as Lord, continue to live in him, ⁷rooted and built up in him, strengthened in the faith as you were taught, and overflowing with thankfulness.

QUESTION ?

In what ways was the world of the Colossian church like our own?

QUESTION ?

What surprises you about the nature of the worldwide church today?

---

wisdom" (Col 1:28);

❱ an aim to "present everyone perfect in Christ" (Col 1:28).

A message for all people

Until the death and resurrection of Jesus, the nations of the world were excluded from his special relationship with Israel – the Jewish people. But Jesus Christ is the pinnacle of God's work in history.

In Jesus, God has made known the 'mystery' to the Gentiles – which is the wonder of "Christ in you all, the hope of glory" (Col 1:27).

Through Christ the nations of the world are to be —

❱ reconciled to God;

❱ offered a hope for the future.

FIRST, THE GOOD NEWS

The worldwide expansion of Christianity in the past 200 years is unprecedented.

There was a time when it could be said – though wrongly – that "Christianity is the white man's religion." But no longer.

❱ Of 4,000 delegates from 186 nations to the Global Consultation on World Evangelism in 1997, only 500 were from North America.

Due to the expansion of missionary outreach in the 19ᵗʰ century, and the establishment and growth of churches worldwide in the 20ᵗʰ century —

❱ In 1900, less than one in five of the world's Christians were non-white. Today, the church is bigger in the Two-Thirds world than it is in the West.

❱ In 1900, Korea was only just open to missionary activity. Now over one in five of the population are actively Christian.

❱ Across sub-Saharan Africa the Christian Church grows at the rate of 65,000 every day.

1
2
3
4
5
6
7
8
9
10
11

BACKGROUND

THE WORLD OF THE COLOSSIANS

Colossae had become a cosmopolitan community. This included —

❖ Phrygians – the natives of the area. Their religion was one of ecstatic nature worship.

❖ Greek settlers, including Epicureans who saw pleasure as the supreme god and goal in life, and thought that death meant extinction.

❖ Stoics, with their emphasis on ethics and knowledge.

The prevailing mood was one of materialism and fatalism due to —

❖ the failure of the old Greco-Roman religion

❖ the moral laxity and intellectual muddle.

This led to —

❖ the outward ceremony of religion having no impact on daily life;

❖ a lack of a personal dimension to religion;

❖ a sense of spiritual rootlessness and despair;

❖ a concentration on material things as the key to happiness.

The answers being proposed by those outside the church included —

❖ demonology;

❖ astrology;

❖ magic;

❖ mystery religions offering deliverance from fate, personal communion with God and assurance of immortality;

❖ gnosis – secret knowledge;

❖ philosophy, notably Epicureanism and Stoicism.

Many, if not all, of these elements are alluded to in some way by Paul in his letter to the Colossians.

> *"It is not my business to think about myself. My business is to think about God. It is for God to think about me."* **Simone Weil**

1 The non-Western church is also a significant missionary
2 force.

3 ▶ The South Korean church is well on the way to a
4 target, set in 1990, to send out 10,000
5 missionaries by the year 2000.
6 ▶ Brazilian missionaries are serving in Europe and
7 beginning to move into North Africa and the
8 Middle East.
9 ▶ The number of native Burmese missionaries is 25
10 times greater than the foreign missionaries
11 excluded in 1966, and some say ten times as
12 effective.
13 ▶ Some 50,000 Indian missionaries are taking the
14 gospel to the sub-continent.
15 ▶ The Ukraine, with 20 theological training
16 projects, is sending missionaries to Russia.
17 ▶ African churches send out 14,494 missionaries,
and host 17,464.
▶ There are 4,000 cross-cultural missionaries from Latin America.

We live at a time when the worldwide fellowship of those who are 'in Christ' is beginning to resemble what is described in the book of Revelation as a "great multitude that no-one could count, from every nation, tribe, people and language".

BACKGROUND

PAUL'S MISSION AND MESSAGE

Although the book of Acts presents Paul as mainly reaching out to the Jews, he saw himself as an apostle to the Gentiles. This can be seen from the churches he founded —

Thessalonians – had turned to God from idols (1 Thes 1:9).

Galatians – had worshipped 'those who are not gods' (Gal 4:8).

Corinthians – had worshipped dumb idols (1 Cor 12:2).

Philippians – were not circumcised (Phil 3:2).

Acts depicts Paul as speaking in the market place. Had he been a philosopher, this is most likely. In Acts 17:17 he also describes his debating partners as philosophers.

Yet Paul obviously tells of other ways than public address. He had a trade and would have talked with customers. He went to where people indicated spiritual awareness.

His basic message was —

❖ the death of Jesus, God's Son

❖ the resurrection of Jesus

❖ the lordship of Jesus Christ

❖ God's judgement – the coming of the end of the age: the end times

❖ the life of those in Christ.

37
38 ## THE NOT-SO-GOOD NEWS
39 The Church worldwide is growing, but there is no
40 room for complacency.
41 ▶ Discipling and training these new Christians is a
42 major task, if they are not to become merely
43 nominal in their adherence to the Christian faith.
44 ▶ The majority of the church growth in Africa is
45 from the children of Christians rather than the
46 result of conversions.
47 ▶ There are indications that church attendance has

declined in South Korea.

If the 'mystery' of the gospel is to be made known to all nations on earth, there is still much to be done. For example —

▶ Almost one-third the world's population has yet to hear the good news about Jesus;

▶ Millions do not have the freedom to speak about Jesus publicly for fear of arrest or harassment;

▶ Hundreds of thousands do not have any portion of the Bible in their own language;

▶ Whole tribes have never even seen a complete Bible, never mind owned one;

▶ In South America there are 30 ministers of the gospel for every million people; in India 15 and in America over 1,400.

Unreached peoples

One-third of the world's population have not only yet to hear the gospel, they do not have a Christian witness living among them.

The Joshua Project 2000 has identified —

▶ 1,739 unreached people groups each with no current ongoing missionary activity among them.

▶ 221 of these people groups have more than a million people each.

▶ Many of these groups live in the 10/40 Window, the historic heartlands of Islam, Hinduism and Buddhism.

A WORLD IN CHANGE
Culture

The mission statement of the Coca Cola Corporation is to see 'a Coke in the hand of every person on earth by

QUESTION ?

What surprises you about the many who have still not heard the good news about Jesus?

PEOPLE GROUP

Jesus gave the instruction to 'make disciples of all nations'. However, the word translated *nation* conveys the sense of *tribe* and *community* rather than those living in a national boundary – which could include many such tribes or people groups.

In the UK this would include those as diverse as gypsies and groups from other ethnic origins as well as those within recognised natural boundaries.

The 10/40 Window

97 per cent of the least evangelized countries of the world are in the 10/40 Window

1
2
3
4
5
6
7
8
9
10
11
12
13
14
15
16
17
18
19
20
21
22
23
24
25
26
27
28
29
30
31
32
33
34
35
36
37
38
39
40
41
42
43
44
45
46
47

1 the year 2000'. At the same time, MTV, McDonald's,
2 Microsoft and Gap are youth symbols worldwide.
3 ▶ Our world is becoming increasingly uniform due
4   to the way Western cultural and economic values
5   are exported to country after country.
6 ▶ The teenagers and twenty-somethings of Tokyo,
7   Sao Paulo, New York, London and Tel Aviv often
8   have more in common with each other than with
9   their parents.
10
11 The key word in the world economy is 'globalization'.
12 For example, the Intel microprocessor in the computer
13 on which these words were first written was designed in
14 California, financed in Germany, made in South Korea
15 and bought in the UK.
16
17 This means that the world 'out there' looks more and
18 more like the one we are familiar with. For example, in
19 Africa —
20 ▶ there is not only rural poverty but also urban
21   growth;
22 ▶ twenty-one cities have a population of over 1
23   million;
24 ▶ Lagos, Nigeria, will soon have a greater
25   population than London.
26
27 In the same way, the stereotypical image of a Muslim as
28 an old man in a turban – standing with a camel on one
29 side and a veiled woman on the other – is no longer
30 true. Instead, think also of an urban teenager.
31

32 Communication revolution

33 Technology and industrialisation have made their global
34 impact. Now the communication revolution is doing
35 the same.
36 ▶ Television sets are found in every African and
37   Indian village.
38 ▶ Satellite dishes clutter the skylines of Teheran and
39   Cairo.
40 ▶ The Internet may still be a Western-dominated
41   medium, but it is growing in use throughout the
42   third world.
43
44 These changes present a real challenge to making the
45 mystery of God's love in Christ known in all the world.
46 Western cultural values have come from —
47 ▶ the growth of cities;

QUESTION ?

What significant changes have come to our world over the last 50 years or so? What relevance do they have to the missionary task of the church?

- the spread of technology;
- the growth of a secular and materialistic world view.

This world – so familiar to us in the West – is the one in which we have struggled to communicate and live out the gospel. We will see the same attitudes and beliefs being lived out around the world.

Despite this universal impact and growth in shared values and experiences, in terms of the role of mission there are still significant differences.

Some communities are —

Pre-Christian – with little or no understanding of the truth about Jesus.

Christianised – with strong churches and a population regularly exposed to Christians and their message.

Post-Christian – where what has become generally a secular population has the residual knowledge and affiliation to the institution of the church, but little perception of its message.

GROWING FUNDAMENTALISM
The world-wide growth in a non-religious attitude to life is not all that is happening. Almost in contradiction, there is a parallel trend.

Religion itself is not dying – but is busy reacting to the impact of Western secular values. The result is the growth of religious fundamentalism.

- In India, the fundamentalist Hindu BJP party is the single biggest political party in parliament.
- In Iran, Egypt, Algeria, Palestine and Afghanistan, among others, Islamic fundamentalism is popular, especially among disenfranchised young people.
- the growth of the Christian church – which is happening in every continent except Western Europe – has mainly come from those who see things in very black and white terms.
- In Indonesia, Muslim militants have destroyed 50 Christian churches.
- In Israel, the Jewish Defence League, a radical

1
2
3
4
5
6
7
8
9
10
11
12
13
14
15
16
17
18
19
20
21
22
23
24
25
26
27
28
29
30
31
32
33
34
35
36
37
38
39
40
41
42
43
44
45
46
47

"The whole church must become a mobile missionary force, ready for a wilderness life. It is a time for us all to be thinking of campaign tents rather than of cathedrals." **John A. MacKay**

FUNDAMENTALISM

Religious movements that —

- ❖ hold unswervingly to the rigid and detailed application of their beliefs;
- ❖ make little or no allowance for the application of what they believe to the understanding of the day;
- ❖ are openly hostile, uncompromising and militant in respect of the culture of the day.

1 group formed by the late messianic Rabbi Meir
2 Kahane, preaches the use of force and violence for
3 liquidation of the exile.
4
5 **THE RICH AND POOR DIVIDE**
6 The first Christians lived in a world where riches and
7 poverty lived side by side. But, in the main, there was
8 no gulf between communities that were either
9 overwhelmingly wealthy or abjectly poor.
10
11 Our world is different. There is a deep and growing gulf
12 between those who are rich and those who are poor.
13 Worse still, those who are rich tend to be so directly at
14 the expense of those who are poor.
15
16 Picture it this way. In an imaginary town of 6,000 —
17 ▶ The richest are among the 860 people who live
18   on the hill overlooking the town.
19 ▶ The remaining 5,140 people live down in the
20   rocky valley bottom.
21
22 Those living on the hill have —
23 ▶ three-quarters of the cars;
24 ▶ 80 per cent of the money;
25 ▶ 80 per cent of the TVs and video.
26
27 The rich folks on the hill also spend —
28 ▶ £200 to protect themselves from the others in the
29   town;
30 ▶ £80 on gambling;
31 ▶ £55 on alcohol;
32 ▶ £35 on tobacco;
33 ▶ £2 to help the 'less fortunate' members of the
34   community.
35
36 Of those in the valley —
37 ▶ One-fifth will die of starvation or related causes
38   before reaching 20 years of age;
39 ▶ They will spend less than two years in school;
40 ▶ They will have one chance in ten of seeing a
41   health worker *in their lifetime*;
42 ▶ They will try to survive on £150 a year.
43
44 This is our world. Those of us who live in the
45 developed world are those who live on the hill. The rest
46 of the world live in the valley. The gulf between them is
47 huge – and growing.

"The spirit of Christ is a spirit of missions and the nearer we get to him, the more intensely missionary we must become." **Henry Martyn**

"Sin is a refusal to submit to the order of things." **Alexis Carrel**

QUESTION ?

In what ways does our lifestyle relate to the message that we are called to share worldwide?

The globalization of the world economy means that the skilled, income- generating planning, design and development work is done up the hill, while production is transferred to wherever wage costs are lowest down in the valley.

Western consumers gain through getting the product of our choice more cheaply. But at the expense of those forced to work for far less than we would be prepared to receive. Our rising standard of living is largely at the expense of the poorest in the world, who grow poorer as we grow richer.

LIVING MORE SIMPLY

To tell people of the love of God but not to demonstrate what that love looks like is hypocrisy of the highest order.

One of the most significant gatherings of world church leaders in recent history put it this way —

> "All of us are shocked by the poverty of millions and disturbed by the injustices which cause it. Those of us who live in affluent circumstances accept our duty to develop a simple lifestyle in order to contribute more generously to both relief and evangelism."
> *From the Lausanne Covenant, 1974.*

People were created to be stewards of the resources that God has given (Gen 1:26–28).

Some people may actually be called to relocate in order to serve the needs of poor people. Others may open their homes to those in need. However, everyone can choose a simpler lifestyle in order to manage on less and give away more.

No rules and regulations can be laid down for this. But we can take seriously the possibilities to —

STATS

PERSONAL LIFESTYLE

Our Christian responsibility demands a lifestyle that avoids waste or selfishness – no matter what the needs of others may be. However, who would wish to live in any other way considering that —

❖ 1,000 million people are destitute;

❖ 10,000 die of starvation every day;

❖ GNP ranges from $80 a year in Mozambique to $40,630 in Switzerland;

❖ Virtually everyone in North Korea is malnourished, and one in five of the 24 million population face imminent death by starvation;

❖ The average child born in the west will eat and drink about 30 times more in their lifetime than a child born in the third world;

❖ Almost a quarter of the world's population lives in poverty;

❖ Of every 1,000 children, 58 die before their fifth birthday.

"Complete possession is proved only by giving. All you are unable to give possesses you." **André Gide**

1   ▶ avoid waste and extravagance – personally and in
2   society as a whole;
3   ▶ choose goods and products that do not damage
4   the resources, environment or lifestyle of others.
5

6 **International perspectives**
7 There are some choices that we have little power over –
8 but this does not mean they can be ignored. These
9 include —
10   ▶ the behaviour of multi-nation companies;
11   ▶ the sale of arms;
12   ▶ international trading structures;
13   ▶ the way wealthy nations handle Third World
14   debt.
15

16 Change will not come through simple living alone.
17 Christians, along with the rest of society, are inevitably
18 involved in politics, which is 'the art of living in
19 community'. To help contribute to change, we can —
20   ▶ pray for peace and justice;
21   ▶ take the trouble to learn more about the moral
22   and political issues;
23   ▶ take action. For example: join the campaign to
24   cancel Third World debt. Contact Jubilee 2000,
25   PO Box 100, London SE1 7RT.
26

27 **REACHING OUT TO THE WORLD**
28 Around us is a vast and needy world – waiting for the
29 good news about Jesus. This means there is a real and
30 ongoing need for serious, long term missions
31 involvement. Previous generations – though not perfect
32 – did a superb job. There is a need for a contemporary
33 response to meet the needs of today.
34

35 **Starting where we are**
36 The church at Colossae came into being as the direct
37 result of the first Christians being obedient to Jesus.
38 They had —
39   ▶ waited in Jerusalem until they received the power
40   of the Holy Spirit (Acts 1:4);
41   ▶ begun to be witnesses to and for Jesus where they
42   were;
43   ▶ gone on to take the same message further afield
44   and to the ends of the earth (Acts 1:8).
45

46 God's strategy for mission is to begin where we are.
47 Effectiveness at home then provides the credentials and

"You are either a missionary or a mission field: one of the two." **Olaf Skinsnes**

"True civilisation does not lie in gas, nor in steam, nor in turn-tables. It lies in the reduction of the traces of original sin." **Charles Baudelaire**

experience for taking the good news about Jesus Christ further afield.

FRUIT AND NUTS

Something as everyday as a bar of Fruit and Nut chocolate can open our eyes to the world of mission.

Cocoa

The cocoa pods come from Malaysia. The plantation is run for the government by Mohammed, who, like most Malays, is a Muslim.

Malaysia is one of the 'Asian Tiger' economies, and its Islamic identity is confident and expansionist.
- The Malaysian prime minister, Mohammed Mahathir, is an exponent of 'Asian values', which is taken by some to be a codeword for strong social conformity.
- Certain religious words, such as God, salvation, heaven, and so on, are only permitted for use by Muslims.

The small Malaysian church is committed to —
- plant 4000 new churches (there are currently around 2300),
- raise up 100,000 prayer partners for Malaysia,
- a programme of leadership training, a vital step if this plan is to succeed.

Mission agencies working in Malaysia include OMF International, and Wycliffe Bible Translators.

Raisins

The raisins come from California, where Joe works in a large vineyard.

Joe's an ordinary guy; think Dan Connor, Homer Simpson, and Hank Hill. He doesn't want much out of life: a bigger house, a newer car, more cable channels, and kids that don't fight.

There are lots of churches in Joe's town. The challenges of consumerism and materialism, which face the church throughout the West, are particularly acute in California, the richest state in the richest nation in the world.

1
2
3
4
5
6
7
8
9
10
11
12
13
14
15
16
17
18
19
20
21
22
23
24
25
26
27
28
29
30
31
32
33
34
35
36
37
38
39
40
41
42
43
44
45
46
47

QUESTION ?

What surprises you about the variety of spiritual deeds set out in the following section?
Which one of them touches your own heart the most?
Why do you think this is?

"There is no argument for missions. The total action of God in history, the whole revelation of God in Christ — this is the argument."
James S. Stewart

"Vox populi, vox humbug."
William Sherman

Nuts

The nuts are picked by Jose in Chile, a South American country 2600 miles long and on average 100 miles wide. Chile —

- is nominally Roman Catholic.
- has seen massive church growth this century, so that 1 Chilean in 4 now calls himself Pentecostal.

The middle and upper classes are being reached by mission organisations such as the South American Mission Society (Anglican), and the Baptists.

There is great need to consolidate this growth.

- Previously successful evangelistic methods, such as street preaching, no longer work as well as they did.
- For the first time, there is evidence that the Pentecostal church has shrunk in size.

Teaching and leadership training are recurring needs. The Chilean church is not yet fulfilling its role in world mission. Its isolation has hindered the growth of a wider outlook.

Paper

Charles manages the export of wood from his hometown of Monrovia, in Liberia on the west coast of Africa. This wood is turned into paper in mills in Britain.

Liberia has suffered immensely in recent years.

- Originally a colony for freed American slaves to be returned to Africa, the resident tribes resented the arrival of the newcomers, who settled in the best land near the coast.
- Tribalism is rife, and a terrible civil war has devastated the country.
- African traditional religions are still very strong, being followed by over half the population, and secret societies and freemasonry are endemic.

As a result of the Civil War —

- There are very few leaders left in the churches. Many were killed or fled.
- There is a desperate need for social and economic reconstruction, and reconciliation between the various tribal groups.

"A priest's life is not supposed to be well-rounded; it is supposed to be one-pointed — a compass, not a weathercock." **Aldous Huxley**

"We'd all like to vote for the best man, but he's never a candidate." **'Kin' Hubbard**

36

Organisations such as Tearfund and SIM International have been heavily involved in Liberia.

Aluminium

The aluminium foil comes from a smelter in the former Soviet republic of Georgia, on the eastern coast of the Black Sea. The country has been Christian since the 4th century, and the Bible was translated into Georgian at that time.

- ▶ Bible translation work is again under way – by both the Orthodox church and the United Bible Societies – as the current version in use was translated 900 years ago.
- ▶ The Georgian Orthodox Church is at the heart of national life, with many being baptised since the fall of Communism, including the president.

Georgian national pride is very strong, This —
- ▶ Alienates the other ethnic minorities within the country, such as Armenians and Azerbaijanis.
- ▶ Makes conversion from the Orthodox church difficult.

There are few evangelicals or missionaries in the country, although a 30 minute Christian radio programme is broadcast to Georgia daily by HCJB Radio (in Ecuador).

Onward to 'Judea' and the ends of the earth

In today's world, 'going further afield' may not be simply a matter of geography. To quote Samuel Escobar, Peruvian theologian and mission leader, "Today, missionaries may have to cross frontiers of a very different kind – cultural frontiers, social frontiers, urban frontiers, spiritual power frontiers, religious frontiers."

It is not always a matter of geography. All around us there are opportunities to make friends with people of other nationalities and faiths.
- ▶ Many would welcome an invitation to a meal.
- ▶ Many immigrants are eager to learn to read and speak English. There is a shortage of Teachers of English as a Foreign Language. A short TEFL training course would provide the link.

"Yes, I see the Church as the body of Christ. But, oh! How we have blemished and scarred that body through social neglect and through fear of being nonconformist." **Martin Luther King, Jr.**

"You're still the king—even in your underwear." **Ludwig Fulda**

1 **REACHING PEOPLE WHERE THEY ARE**

2 **Pray**

3 Prayer is fueled by information. This means finding out
4 about a country's —
5 ▶ specific needs and problems; ·
6 ▶ percentage of the population that are Christians;
7 ▶ which mission agencies work there.

9 The way to gain the background for prayer is to—
10 ▶ Send away to some of these missionary societies
11 for more information.
12 ▶ Get a copy of *Operation World*, which gives facts
13 and figures about each country in the world.
14 ▶ Adopt a missionary, perhaps with others in your
15 house group, and commit yourself to regular
16 prayer for them.

18 **Give**

19 It is said that American Christians spend more on pet
20 food in 52 days than they give in a year to foreign
21 mission! Those in the UK are probably little different.
22 ▶ If your church supports mission, perhaps you
23 could give an additional gift and earmark it for a
24 named missionary or a specific project.
25 ▶ Over and above your regular giving, you could
26 send a small, regular amount to some special
27 overseas concern.
28 ▶ You could send a special parcel of 'goodies' to
29 encourage a missionary. But you will need to
30 check first with a missionary society that works in
31 the area, in case there are local regulations to be
32 aware of.

34 **Write**

35 A letter to a missionary will give pleasure far beyond all
36 the time and energy you put into writing it.

38 **Go**

39 "Are you ready, if God calls, not only to look out but
40 also to go out? God will be calling some of you reading
41 this to work overseas. I pray that you will hear and
42 respond to his call." Stephen Gaukroger, *Making it*
43 *Work*, Scripture Union.

45 **Working where they live**

46 It is possible to work abroad —
47 ▶ **modelling the Christian faith** – by example and

> *"Its name is Public Opinion. It is held in reverence. It settles everything. Some think it is the voice of God."* **Mark Twain**

> *"Action is the proper fruit of knowledge."* **Thomas Fuller**

service;

- **using business skills** – in training programmes to promote Christian ethics in business, or setting up income-generating programmes that contribute to community development and the funding of Christian ministry and mission.

Such workers are sometimes referred to as 'tentmakers' (see Acts 18:3). They —

- are self-supporting and not in need of financial backing from their home church;
- can live and work in countries to which traditional missionaries are denied access.

Going where they are

It is possible to be sent as a missionary – through the support of a mission agency and/or sending church. This makes it possible to be involved full time in evangelism, church planting, education, medicine or relief and development work.

The key to effectiveness in mission for the future will be in partnerships. This includes —

- UK churches partnering together to reach out cross-culturally;
- churches partnering with mission agencies;
- churches partnering with churches overseas.

Such partnerships —

- reduce overlap and competition;
- increase effectiveness through each partner playing to their strengths.

This strategic stewardship of resources, people, knowledge and experience is essential if the gospel is to go into all the world.

Being a missionary to mission

Helping others to catch the vision for mission is a very positive role to play. Many mission agencies can provide you with ideas and help. Examples include —

- Organise a shoe shine inititiative with your church, reflecting the plight of hundreds of shoe shine boys in India.
- Organise an Indian meal, giving out literature, showing videos and updating those who attend on what is happening across that nation. Chinese

"Still water and still religion freeze quickest." **Anon**

QUESTION ?

What one action could you take to speed up the spread of the good news worldwide?

1	food could be used for China, North African
2	food for Morocco and so on.
3	
4	
5	
6	
7	
8	
9	
10	
11	
12	
13	
14	
15	
16	
17	
18	
19	
20	
21	
22	
23	
24	

TRAVEL LOG

On my visit to the far country of World Mission —

The most interesting thing I saw was ....

....

....

The most surprising thing I saw was ....

....

....

The most important thing I saw was ....

....

....

Because of my visit, in the future I want to try to ....

....

....

FALSE TEACHING
– THE MINEFIELD

Not everything you hear about God and his message is necessarily true. So how do we know? And then what?

COLOSSIANS 2:8

False teachers were influencing the Christians in the Colossian church – which was the main reason for Paul's letter. Paul warns against these teachers, and argues against their errors. In a very strong warning (v.8) he speaks about:

Their aim – to take the Colossians captive. The picture is of people who plunder the church, carrying some away from the truth into the slavery of error.

Their methods – to try to ensnare the congregation through 'hollow and deceptive philosophy'. They call it philosophy to give it a ring of sophistication and authority. But in reality it is a hollow sham, false and without value.

The foundation of their teaching is 'human tradition'. They claimed an ancient pedigree for their teaching, and therefore a divine origin for their revelations. In reality it had all the hallmarks of human frailty and error – and stood in stark contrast to the truth of the gospel which depended solely on Christ.

The ultimate source of the teaching is 'the basic principles of this world'. The actual phrase that Paul uses here has been much debated, and it is not possible to be absolutely certain what he was referring to.

Two of the main possibilities are:

▶ **Elementary or rudimentary religious teaching** – perhaps pre-Christian religion, whether Jewish or Gentile, and therefore those powers of sin, law and flesh which can only lead to condemnation.

▶ **The elemental spirits of the universe**, ie. the principalities and powers referred to in 2:15.

The church at Colossae was beginning to take on board ideas and teachings from a variety of sources. These included —

▶ Traditional Greek philosophy – ancient traditional teachings of, eg. the Epicureans and Stoics (2:8).

▶ The so-called mystery religions – offering secret initiation into higher knowledge (2:18).

▶ The beginnings of what later became Gnosticism

FULLNESS

This word denotes 'completeness'. It was used to describe the full complement of a ship's crew needed to successfully set sail and finish the voyage.

The implication is that there is absolutely nothing lacking of God in Jesus. There could be no more 'complete' Saviour than him.

⁸See to it that no one takes you captive through hollow and deceptive philosophy, which depends on human tradition and the basic principles of this world rather than on Christ.

AN OVERVIEW OF COLOSSIANS CHAPTER 2

Chapter 2 is mainly a reminder of —

❖ what God has done through Jesus Christ;

❖ the implications of the Colossians' experience of Christ;

❖ a warning against other teachings which, compared with the gospel, are empty and futile.

Paul wants the Colossians to understand that they should not add 'extras' to their life in Christ. Instead, they are to discover and experience more deeply the full understanding of all that is true about Christ (vv.1–5).

The three themes of this chapter are that —

Fullness is found only in Christ. In him "all the **fullness** of the Deity lives in bodily form" (v.9). Therefore, to know Christ, to be joined to him, is to receive —

❖ "fullness" as a gift (v.10);

❖ fullness of forgiveness (v.13);

❖ fullness of resurrection life, as symbolised in baptism, (vv.12–13);

❖ fullness of knowledge and understanding (vv.2–3).

Freedom is experienced only in Christ. The Christian is set free from —

❖ the deadness of the past (v.13);

❖ the old sinful nature (v.11);

WORLD MISSION FAMILY THE WORLD OF WORK SPIRITUAL WARFARE 7

– combining ideas from the mystery religions with Christian teaching to offer 'fullness' (1:19; 2:9).

▶ Paganism, in the form of astrology, magic and demonology – the need to placate the 'powers', overcome one's fate written in the stars, perhaps through 'worship of angels' (2:8,18,20,23).

▶ Paganism, in the form of immorality and low ethical standards (3:5–11);

▶ Judaism, or perhaps legalistic Jewish Christians – insisting on rules and regulations for every part of life (2:20–23).

The church at Colossae was part of a multi-cultural, ethnically diverse and religiously pluralist society. And it was all too easy for them to take on board ideas and practises which should have no place within the one true gospel uniquely revealed in Christ.

THE CREEDS

It was because of the influence of false teaching that the early church created creeds – statements of formal belief.

The first creeds were relatively simple. But they became increasingly longer as more error needed to be refuted.

One of the earliest creeds – that of Cyprian of Carthage – said simply —

I believe in God the Father
in Christ his Son
in the Holy Spirit and the remission of sins and life
everlasting through the Holy Church.

Another typical early creed responded to —

▶ claims that Jesus came only as a spirit and only appeared to be flesh, which denies Christ's humanity and, effectively, our redemption.

▶ claims that the resurrection was only spiritual.

It read —

I believe in God the Father almighty
And in Jesus Christ his only Son our Lord
Who was born of the Holy Spirit and the Virgin Mary
Who was crucified under Pontius Pilate and was buried
On the third day he rose again from the dead

1
2
3
4
5
6
7
8
9
10
11
12
13
14
15
16
17
18
19
20
21
22
23
24
25
26
27
28
29
30
31
32
33
34
35
36
37
38
39
40
41
42
43
44
45
46
47

QUESTION ?

Can you think of ways in which the church in the UK has been influenced just as the church at Colossae was?

❖ condemnation (v.14);

❖ the powers (v.15);

❖ man-made regulations (v.20).

Freedom is one of the great hallmarks of that "reality … found in Christ" (v.17). Therefore the Colossians are to make sure that they do not become captive to the false teachings which were being presented to them. These teachings were by definition -

❖ false (vv.18, 23);

❖ feeble – "lack any value in restraining sensual indulgence" (v.23);

❖ ultimately futile – "empty and hollow" (v.8).

Focus must be fully on Christ (vv.6–7). Everything they could ever need in this life and the life to come is to be found in Christ. Therefore, the Colossians must "continue to live in him".

This means "to acknowledge his lordship and rule in everything". Not only in the once-for-all decision of conversion. But as the overarching principle and undergirding foundation of their whole lives.

Individually and together they are to become ever more strongly committed to the faith they have been taught. For it is this focus that will effectively guard them against the errors that bombard them.

"Innocence comes in contact with evil and doesn't know it; it baffles temptation; it is protected where no one else is." **Basil W.Maturin**

> *"Error makes the circuit of the globe while truth is pulling on her boots."*
> **Orestes Brownson**

1 *Ascended into heaven*
2 *Sat at the right hand of the Father*
3 *And will come again to judge the living and the dead*
4 *And in the Holy Spirit*
5 *Holy Church*
6 *The remission of sins*
7 *The resurrection of the body.*
8 *(Roman Creed – c. 200)*
9

10 ERROR IN THE CHURCH TODAY

11 Some sectors of the worldwide church have become
12 deeply infected with error. These include beliefs that —
13 ▶ Jesus was not divine;
14 ▶ God is no longer intimately involved with his
15 world;
16 ▶ In order to be accepted by God it is necessary to
17 keep a set of rules and regulations.
18

19 Error is also to be found in the section of the church
20 that regards itself as being faithful to the teaching of the
21 Bible. Such false teaching includes beliefs that —
22 ▶ Some teaching is the result of God's special
23 revelation;
24 ▶ God's plan is always to heal Christians of all
25 illness;
26 ▶ It is necessary for Christians to keep the Jewish
27 food laws and to observe the festivals of the Old
28 Testament;
29 ▶ God rewards the faithfulness of his children by
30 blessing them with personal wealth.
31

32 KEEPING ERROR OUT OF THE CHURCH

33 Many atrocities have been committed under the guise
34 of keeping the teaching of the church free from error –
35 including burning 'heretics' at the stake.
36

37 In contrast, in our more liberal age, it takes courage to
38 dare to say that anyone else is 'wrong' on a religious
39 matter. One cynic put it, "We include the Devil as a
40 fourth person of the Trinity so as not to offend the local
41 Satanists."
42

43 The most effective way to keep out error is to teach
44 truth. C H Spurgeon, the great Baptist preacher, said,
45 "If you want to see if a stick is bent, put a straight one
46 against it."
47

[9]For in Christ all the fullness of the Deity lives in bodily form, [10]and you have been given fullness in Christ, who is the head over every power and authority. [11]In him you were also circumcised, in the putting off of the sinful nature,[7] not with a circumcision done by the hands of men but with the circumcision done by Christ, [12]having been buried with him in baptism and raised with him through your faith in the power of God, who raised him from the dead.

[13]When you were dead in your sins and in the uncircumcision of your sinful nature,[8] God made you[9] alive with Christ. He forgave us all our sins, [14]having cancelled the written code, with its regulations, that was against us and that stood opposed to us; he took it away, nailing it to the cross.

QUESTION ?

What helps you to avoid error in what you believe?

[7] 11 Or *the flesh*
[8] 13 Or *your flesh*
[9] 13 Some manuscripts *us*

This makes it vital to —
- include relevant systematic theology within the teaching programme of the local church;
- teach about cults and sects;
- describe world religions in the light of the Bible;
- be alert.

CULTS AND SECTS

As well as the error that surfaces within the church, there is also the false teaching just outside the door. This error comes from movements close to the church but not quite in it.

Those involved are generally called *cults* or *sects*. A more recent name is *New Religious Movements* (NRMs).

NRMs are usually very sharply defined. You are either 'in' or 'out', and great emphasis is placed on everyone toeing the party line on doctrine and behaviour.

A number of consistent characteristics are often present and help to identify an NRM:
- Special interpretation of and insights into the Bible.
- Additions to the Bible or their own version of it.
- Syncretistic origins. i.e. they are often a hotchpotch of Christian faith and popular folk religions – like Christian Science.
- A faulty understanding of the nature of Christ – 'fully God and fully Man' – and with regard to the Trinity – like Unitarians.
- Messianic leaders who instruct the faithful – like "Jim" Jones and the Jonestown mass suicide in northwestern Guyana by members of the People's Temple.
- Certainty, emotional assurance and zeal in holding their convictions like David Koresh in Waco, Texas.
- Exclusivism – claiming to be the only way to God – like Jehovah's Witnesses.
- Emphasis on the End Times and how they will unfold – like the Heaven's Gate Halebop comet group who killed themselves.
- Psychological pressure to stay within the group or to lose your salvation by backsliding or joining less 'sound' groups – like the London Church of Christ.

"An old error is always more popular than a new truth."
German proverb

"There is no Christianity without the practice of it."
John R. de Witt

1 ▶ Signs and wonders, especially for those who have
2 had a mystical experience of some kind – like the
3 Children of God.
4
5 The NRMs are of relevance to Christians for two
6 reasons —
7 ▶ their false teaching needs to be kept out of the
8 church;
9 ▶ they deserve to be delivered from error.
10

TELLING THOSE IN ERROR THE TRUTH

It is not easy to help those in NRMs find real faith in
Jesus. This is particularly because many see themselves
as the 'true' Christian Church.
▶ Many members of NRMs joined because they
failed to find anything relevant in the church.
▶ Others have been given a very distorted picture of
genuine Christian belief.

We have the opportunity to show them the love and life
of Christ.

Rather than arguing detailed aspects of their belief, it is
better to be a witness to all that Jesus is doing for us
and in the life of the church. Our personal experience is
a strong place to start.

THE SPIRIT OF THE AGE
The influence of Christian belief
The world outside the church is busy 'being' and
'doing'. This includes forming opinions as to what is
true and right. And the voice of the church plays its
part in shaping these opinions.

The teaching of the Bible and the prophetic voice of
the church have shaped Western culture more than
anything else in the last two millennia. This accounts
for the beliefs of the older generation
regarding marriage, honesty, the work
ethic and so on.

The influence of society on the church
There are times when it would seem
that God uses human culture to cause
Christians to think again – and so to
refine our beliefs and practices.

"It is one thing to show a man that he is in error, and another to put him in possession of truth." **John Locke**

STATS

ADDITIONS TO THE BIBLE
❖ The Book of Mormon for the Church of Jesus Christ of the Latter Day Saints;
❖ The Divine Principle for the Unification Church;
❖ Dianetics for Scientology;
❖ The sermons of William Branham for Branhamites/Oneness Pentecostals.

This can be seen over issues like —   1
- ▶ the treatment of slaves;   2
- ▶ the role of women;   3
- ▶ the government of the church;   4
- ▶ relations with the state;   5
- ▶ divorce;   6
- ▶ pollution of the environment;   7
- ▶ contraception;   8
- ▶ the language of worship;   9
- ▶ the general availability of the Bible;   10
- ▶ and much more.   11
                                                                        12
In each of these cases – and many others – it was the   13
world at large that caused the church to rethink its   14
assumptions.   15
                                                                        16
This makes it important to evaluate with care the voices   17
that whisper – and sometimes shout – in the ear of the   18
church. The prevailing view of society is not the basis   19
on which the church is to make up its mind. But   20
sometimes we need to listen and re-examine the Bible   21
to find out what it really means.   22
                                                                        23
Nevertheless, it is all too easy for beliefs and attitudes   24
from our secular culture to influence us.   25
                                                                        26
Such influences can include —   27
- ▶ **our values** – what we hold to be important;   28
- ▶ **our morals** – how we believe it is right to behave;   29
- ▶ **our worldview** – our beliefs as to what is true and   30
  real.   31
                                                                        32
In every case, such error in the church will damage our   33
understanding of the supremacy of Christ and our   34
effectiveness as his disciples.   35
                                                                        36
The influences from the spirit of our own age that   37
threaten us include —   38
                                                                        39
Non-rationality   40
Many in our society have lost any notion of there being   41
a Big Picture – that history has any shape or destiny.   42
The great hopes offered by political systems, education,   43
affluence and the rest no longer hold water. The   44
competing philosophies are just a pick-and-mix   45
smorgasbord.   46
                                                                        47

QUESTION ?

Make a list of several issues where the church has been rightly influenced by society in recent years. List some issues on which the church may have yet to listen.

"Man is prone to connect the idea of innocence with that of abstention. There are, however, abstentions which are crimes." **Ernest Hello**

"Attempt great things for God; expect things from God." **William Carey**

1 The result has also been an emphasis on feelings and
2 intuition at the expense of logic. What we 'feel' has
3 become more valid than what seems reasonable.
4
5 Christians can fall for the same trap – with experience
6 being regarded as the pinnacle of discipleship.
7
8 Instead, Christian response ought to defend rationality
9 and the power of verbal communication. It is the Word
10 made flesh who gives us our Big Picture. But this brings
11 the danger of exalting reason above God and
12 denigrating the intuitive and emotional.
13
14 The New Testament gives the mind an important place
15 in Christian life and experience. Conversion involves
16 repentance (the Greek word means 'a change of mind').
17 Growth in maturity and moral living requires a renewal
18 of the mind (Rom 12:1,2; Eph 4:23; Col 3:10). The
19 mind should be *engaged* in worship (1 Cor 14:13–15).
20
21 **Consumerism**
22 In contrast to what Jesus taught, we are led to believe
23 that our significance stems from the sum total of all
24 that we own. That it is in choosing and in buying that
25 we find identity and acceptance. *Tesco, ergo sum* – I
26 shop, therefore I am.
27
28 Our society offers a choice of 83 different breakfast
29 cereals and new fashion for every season. This is the
30 illusion of freedom which capitalism offers us. It builds
31 on the premise that 'the love of money' is the only
32 dynamism by which the world economy can function.
33
34 Christians, individually and as communities, can find
35 themselves operating on the same basis – inside and
36 outside of the church. For example —
37 ▶ Do we choose our church on the same basis as we
38 do our supermarket?
39 ▶ Is our church a place where we want a return for
40 our investment?
41 ▶ Is what the church has more important than what
42 it is?
43
44 **Deadening of Feelings**
45 Our TV culture means we have to cope with so many
46 emotions in so short a space of time each day. And the
47 sound-bite sensations have coarsened the human spirit.

*"Evil is unspectacular and always human,
And shares our bed and eats at our own table."*
W.H.Auden

"The Church exists by mission as a fire exists by burning." **Emil Brunner**

QUESTION ?

In what ways has the lie of consumerism – that our identity and acceptance are based on what we own – infected the church?

As a result, the ability to feel deep emotion is spasmodic and brief in today's society. Edward Munch's famous painting *The Scream* is a wonderful expression of the great themes of alienation, boredom, solitude, social fragmentation and isolation that exist in our society.

The impact on the church is the danger of cramming as many emotional experiences as possible into the times we meet for worship. Rather than this liturgical channel-hopping, there is a need to give time and space in our worship for the right use of our senses and emotions.

Loss of Certainty

We live in an age that is suspicious of too much certainty.

This can have its impact in two contrasting ways —
- ▶ We can find ourselves feeling uncomfortable over things where there is no reason for doubt.
- ▶ We can be blindly dogmatic at times when a truly biblical faith should create humility and a degree of provisional uncertainty on us – in case we become proud.

During the past age of reason, the traditional and logical arguments for the truth of Christianity were effective. This approach still works with some people – but it may become increasingly irrelevant to Western society.

We need to let God touch people's hearts and imaginations before we begin to work on their minds.

WORLD RELIGIONS

A World Religion is a religion that most people have heard of – Christianity, Hinduism, Buddhism, Judaism, Islam, for example.

What are we to make of religions that embrace billions of the world's population? Popular wisdom, as displayed on TV chat shows, paints as bigots those who say, 'Not all roads lead to God'.

It is certainly true that all religions cannot be right, as they disagree with each other on so many central issues like —

"I have met many that would deceive; who would be deceived, no one." **Saint Augustine**

"We are born to action; and whatever is capable of suggesting and guiding action has power over us from the first." **Charles Horton Cooley**

1 ▶ what God is like;
2 ▶ the nature of sin;
3 ▶ how forgiveness is possible – and even if it is
4   needed;
5 ▶ what heaven is like – and even if there is such a
6   place.
7
8 Some world religions even disagree on issues like this
9 among themselves.
10
11 Faced with other major religions, Christians have
12 tended to adopt one of two extremes.
13 ▶ All other religions are totally wrong, misguided,
14   deceptive and satanic. All their adherents will
15   certainly go to hell.
16 ▶ It doesn't really matter what you believe, as long
17   as you believe it sincerely. We'll all end up in
18   heaven at the end
19
20 Neither of these does justice to the teaching of the Bible
21 – which stresses honest seeking, merciful and just living
22 and walking in the light that has been given (Matt 7;
23 Micah 6:8; Rom 2).
24
25 As we respond to those who are sincerely wrong, we
26   should remember —

▶ they may not be wrong about everything;

▶ Jesus is the complete revelation of the Truth, and those from other faiths – as well as those with no faith – deserve to hear about him;

▶ people of other faiths are not our enemies. They are our neighbours whom Christ loves and wants to know.

Wherever possible we should look for common ground on which we can build bridges to Christ. It is usually better to concentrate on this than on pointing out their 'error'.

For example, Christians and Muslims have much in common on issues like morality and law and order.

"Few men ever drop dead from overwork, but many quietly curl up and die because of undersatisfaction."
Sydney J.Harris

TRAVEL LOG

On my visit to the minefield of False Teaching —

The most interesting thing I saw was ....

....

....

The most surprising thing I saw was ....

....

....

The most important thing I saw was...............................

....

....

Because of my visit, in the future I want to try to ....

....

....

SPIRITUAL WARFARE

– BATTLE ZONE

The fight is on – against an enemy we cannot see. And using weapons we cannot touch. But the ultimate result is already decided.

COLOSSIANS 2:15

1
2
3 **E**mphasising the victory of Jesus over the
4 principalities and powers, Paul uses graphic terms
5 taken from the military world of the 1ST century.
6
7 He uses three pictures:
8
9 God 'disarmed the powers and authorities'. The main
10 idea here is of the triumphant military commander
11 stripping the defeated enemies of their weapons. The
12 same word was also used of officials in the royal court
13 being disgraced by being publicly stripped of their
14 dignity.
15
16 God 'made a public spectacle of them' – in the same
17 way as defeated soldiers were paraded before the
18 population. In the cross God has shown to the whole
19 universe the true character of the powers. They are
20 helpless, pathetic, even ridiculous.
21
22 God 'triumphed over them'. This is the language of a
23 Roman victory procession – with the defeated enemies
24 being paraded through the streets of the city. God
25 makes clear the powerlessness of these powers and the
26 completeness of his victory over them.
27
28 Paul realised that Jesus' apparent defeat was the
29 moment of ultimate spiritual triumph.

BACKGROUND

JESUS AND SPIRITUAL OPPOSITION

- ❖ Evil spirit confronts Jesus – Mark 1:24, Luke 4:33
- ❖ Jesus casts out Legion – Matt 8:28, Mark 5:2, Luke 8:26
- ❖ Jesus mother calls him mad – Mark 3:21
- ❖ Jesus cannot perform miracles – Mark 6:5, Luke 9:53
- ❖ Peter is called Satan – Matt 16:23, Mark 8:33
- ❖ Satan enters Judas – Luke 22:3 (cf Matt 26:14, Mark 14:10)
- ❖ Jesus escapes – Luke 4:30, John 10:39
- ❖ Jesus hides – John 11:54
- ❖ The disciples fall asleep – Matt 26:36, Mark 14:65, Luke 22:43
- ❖ Satan asked Jesus to give him Simon – Luke 22:31
- ❖ Jesus protected his disciples – John 17:12

Jesus became the atoning sacrifice for our sin, defeated the power of death and overcame the might of human political and religious power. The power of self-giving, divine love overcame – once for all – the demonic hordes of self-interest and hatred.

The New Testament leaves no room for uncertainty. There's a war on. Christians are soldiers fighting spiritual enemies with spiritual weapons.

Paul describes conversion as our rescue "from the dominion of darkness" (Col 1:13).

15And having disarmed the powers and authorities, he made a public spectacle of them, triumphing over them by the cross.[10]

16Therefore do not let anyone judge you by what you eat or drink, or with regard to a religious festival, a New Moon celebration or a Sabbath day. 17These are a shadow of the things that were to come; the reality, however, is found in Christ. 18Do not let anyone who delights in false humility and the worship of angels disqualify you for the prize. Such a person goes into great detail about what he has seen, and his unspiritual mind puffs him up with idle notions. 19He has lost connection with the Head, from whom the whole body, supported and held together by its ligaments and sinews, grows as God causes it to grow.

20Since you died with Christ to the basic principles of this world, why, as though you still belonged to it, do you submit to its rules: 21"Do not handle! Do not taste! Do not touch!"? 22These are all destined to perish with use, because they are based on human commands and teachings. 23Such regulations indeed have an appearance of wisdom, with their self-imposed worship, their false humility and their harsh treatment of the body, but they lack any value in restraining sensual indulgence.

Rules for Holy Living

3 Since, then, you have been raised with Christ, set your hearts on things above, where Christ is seated at the right hand of God. ²Set your minds on things above, not on earthly things. ³For you died, and your life is now hidden with Christ in God. ⁴When Christ, who is your[11] life, appears, then you also will appear with him in glory.

⁵Put to death, therefore, whatever belongs to your earthly nature: sexual immorality, impurity, lust, evil desires and greed, which is idolatry. ⁶Because of these, the wrath of God is coming.[12] ⁷You used to walk in these ways, in the life you once lived. ⁸But now you must rid yourselves of all such things as these: anger, rage, malice, slander, and filthy language from your lips. ⁹ Do not lie to each other, since you have taken off your old self with its practices ¹⁰ and have put on the new self, which is being renewed in knowledge in the image of its Creator. ¹¹ Here there is no Greek or Jew, circumcised or uncircumcised, barbarian, Scythian, slave or free, but Christ is all, and is in all.

QUESTION ?

What surprises you about the issue of spiritual warfare as set out in this section?

---

¹⁰ 15 Or *them in him*

¹¹ 4 Some manuscripts *our*

¹² 6 Some early manuscripts *coming on those who are disobedient*

The first Christians recognised that, behind the various kinds of human opposition, the forces of darkness were at work.

When Paul wrote to the Ephesian Christians, he mentioned —
- 'spiritual forces of evil in the heavenly realms';
- the Christian struggle "against the rulers, against the authorities, against the powers of this dark world" (Eph 6:12).

Paul was not referring to human authorities, because he had just stated that "our struggle is not against flesh and blood" (Eph 6:12).

He had a clear understanding of what had really been behind his experience in Ephesus (Acts 19:24ff), where the silversmiths who were making a living out of selling pagan trinkets rose up to attack Paul and his companions. They could see that the spread of Christian convictions could destroy their business.

These spiritual forces include not only those that once ruled our life, but also the 'world system' that is under the enemy's rule. National life, business life and the structures of institutions can all come under an influence that is greater than the sum total of the badness of the people involved.

This can be seen —
- in the frequent bias of many institutions and organisations towards racism, sexism and the exploitation of the weak;
- in the love of power and self-interest that replace the love of neighbour in political systems;
- at its most extreme, in the adulation and willing obedience that many ordinary people offered to Hitler.

Our response is not as individuals

BACKGROUND

FIRST CHRISTIANS AND SPIRITUAL OPPOSITION

- ❖ The people are accused of being stiff-necked – Acts 7:51
- ❖ Stephen is stoned – Acts 7:57,58
- ❖ Persecution starts – Acts 8:1
- ❖ Evil spirits are cast out – Acts 8:7
- ❖ Jews incite opposition to Paul – Acts 13:50, 14:5, 14:19, 17:13, 18:6,12, 21:28, 23:12
- ❖ Possessed slave girl, shouting, follows Paul for many days – Acts 16:17
- ❖ Hearers refuse to believe – Acts 19:19
- ❖ Riot in Ephesus – Acts 19:23
- ❖ Quarrels among believers – I Cor 1:11
- ❖ Sexual immorality among believers – I Cor 5:1
- ❖ Lawsuits among believers – I Cor 6:7
- ❖ Severe trials – II Cor 8:2
- ❖ Different spirit – II Cor 11:4
- ❖ Deserting Christ – Gal 1:6
- ❖ Bewitched believers – Gal 3:1, 4:9
- ❖ Persecution and trials – II Thes 1:4
- ❖ Handed over to Satan – I Tim 1:20
- ❖ Paul deserted – II Tim 1:15
- ❖ Rebellious people, deceivers – Titus 1:10
- ❖ Godless men – Jude 1:4

1
27
28
29
30
31
32
33
34
35
36
37
38
39
40
41
42
43
44
45
46
47

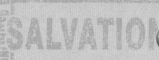
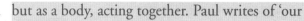

1 but as a body, acting together. Paul writes of 'our
2 struggle' (Eph 6:12). The united force of righteousness
3 is to stand against the systems of darkness.
4

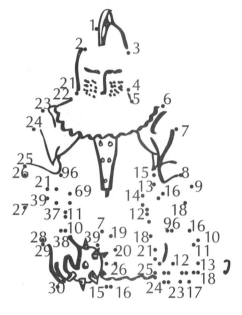

We are not to run or hide. Nor wait for the Lord Jesus to come back. But, together, to fight.

At the same time, we should remember it is the systems that are our enemy, not the people within them.

Spiritual warfare – through prayer and righteous action – is seen in how Christians responded to —

❱ the injustice of unemployment – starting the first labour exchanges
❱ those seeking the safety of asylum in the UK – providing support
❱ those exploited in the developing countries – by working for fair trade.

THE IMPACT OF EVIL

It is comfortable to be able to blame someone else for our human failings. However, it is not unreasonable to believe that it takes some outside wickedness of great size to produce circumstances in which atrocities could take place. Things like —

❱ My Lai massacre on 16 March, 1968, in South Vietnam by Charlie Company, 11th Brigade, led by Lt. William Calley. The slaughter of over 100 unarmed children, women and elderly civilians.
❱ The Armenian Genocide of Word War I, which left 3 out of every 4 Armenian Turks dead at the hands of Turks and Kurds. Over 1.5 million were killed.
❱ The Holocaust of World War II, in which the Germans sought systematically to eradicate the Jewish race. More than 6 million were killed.
❱ Pol Pot, head of the Khmer Rouge from 1968, oversaw the slaughter of hundreds of thousands of Cambodians.

Paul explains that the reason for the growth and power

Take a few moments to complete this dot-to-dot.

What does the experience illustrate about the issue of spiritual warfare?

QUESTION ?

What else could explain these atrocities, other than there being an evil force in the world?

of corruption, immorality and anti-Christian values is two-fold.

> ◗ They are the consequences of our sinfulness as fallen beings (Rom 1:18–32).
> ◗ They are influenced by a demonic infiltration, contamination and distortion that is to be found within the very fabric of human society.

This means that —
> ◗ every society is open to contamination;
> ◗ every organisation will face corrupting pressures;
> ◗ no institution – including the church – is free from the temptation to embrace the love of power rather than self-giving love.

All this is in addition to the impact that dark forces can have on individuals.

UNDERSTANDING THE CONTEXT

It is important to understand that Paul does not write out of fear, but out of confidence. However, Paul sees it as naive if we fail to understand the power, presence and strategies of our enemy.

Personal activity

The first recorded miracle of Jesus that is recorded in Mark's gospel was when he brought deliverance to a demon-possessed man at the synagogue in Capernaum (Mark 1:21–27).

As a result, the people marvelled at Jesus' remarkable authority – 'He even gives orders to evil spirits and they obey him.'

It was therefore inevitable that many people brought not only the sick but the demonized to Jesus (Mark 1:32). They knew that he had the spiritual power to rescue those enmeshed in terrifying spiritual bondage.

Matthew records that Jesus expelled the demons 'with a word' (Matt 8:16).

As we read the Gospels, we can identify several symptoms of demonic possession.
> ◗ Some people fell to the ground in something like an epileptic fit. One young victim's life was often put at risk by his falling into fires and water

"The fox that waited for the chickens to fall off their perch died of hunger." **Greek proverb**

"All sin tends to be addictive, and the terminal point of addiction is what is called damnation." ***W.H.Auden***

1 (Matt 17:15).
2 ▶ This does not mean that epilepsy is a symptom of
3   demonization. In the Scriptures people fall to the
4   ground because of demonization, illness, attack
5   by humans or wild animals, accidents and also as
6   a result of divine visitation. So, in itself, the
7   posture proves nothing.
8 ▶ Others exhibited extravagant violence, terrorising
9   a neighbourhood and driving others away from
10   their solitary haunts (Matt 8:28).
11 ▶ Others declared the truth about Jesus' identity as
12   the Son of God, but in a way that went beyond
13   the limits of ordinary human knowledge
14   (Mark 1:24).
15
16 The New Testament never suggests that any of these
17 symptoms establish a definite diagnosis of
18 demonization. There is always a need for wise, pastoral
19 and spiritual discernment.
20
21 The Apostle Paul reveals a further symptom of spiritual
22 illness – an instinctive cursing and hatred of the name
23 of Jesus (1 Cor 12:3).
24

PATTERNS OF SPIRITUAL OPPOSITION
Direct confrontation

27 The Gospels present three main strands of spiritual
28 confrontation —
29   ▶ the temptations of Jesus;
30   ▶ the outbursts of the demonized;
31   ▶ the gathering opposition that resulted in Jesus'
32   trial and crucifixion.
33
34 The general principle is clear – whenever God's
35 kingdom advances in power, spiritual opposition
36 intensifies.
37
38 For example —
39   ▶ After Jesus' baptism came a time of intense
40   temptation – when Satan pushed him as hard as
41   possible (Matt 4:1–11; Mark 1:12–13).
42   ▶ Throughout Jesus' public activity, demons could
43   not keep silent (Matt 7:36; Mark 3:11–12; Mark
44   5:7; Luke 4:41).
45
46 In the book of Acts this pattern continues. As the
47 Christian leaders moved from place to place, they were

QUESTION ?

◀ How have you seen this demonstrated in your life and the life of your church?

met with demonic activity through the lives and lips of others.

TRAPS TO AVOID

Faced with the subject of spiritual warfare, three kinds of extremism are possible.

Cynicism: Hysterical over-reaction and sheer superstitious foolishness by past generations can lead to us dismissing the supernatural dark side wholesale.

The seemingly sophisticated modern mind can easily treat talk of possession and infiltration as primitive, ridiculous, deluded and even dangerous.

Such an approach ignores significant moments in the life of Christ and the mission of the early church.

Obsession: It is possible to be so focussed on the issue that we begin to see —
- demons behind every sneeze,
- possessions behind every sin and
- principalities behind every disappointment or hardship.

Those who give the devil the 'credit' for every problem or misadventure may be well-intentioned, but far from the truth. For example, while the Apostle Paul was in prison and facing imminent martyrdom, he wrote to the Philippians. But his letter does not utter a single word about spiritual warfare.

Either the obsessives are more spiritual than the Apostle Paul. Or they over- emphasise an aspect of New Testament teaching that is given relatively minor emphasis.

Speculation: Some have treated the brief statements and metaphors in the New Testament concerning demons and spiritual warfare as a gold mine for fanciful and elaborate pronouncements.

The result has been —
- complex charts of the hierarchies of hell;
- detailed diagrams of the demonic infiltration of human society;
- the revelation of methods of spiritual warfare

1
2
3
4
5
6
7
8
9
10
11
12
13
14
15
16
17
18
19
20
21
22
23
24
25
26
27
28
29
30
31
32
33
34
35
36
37
38
39
40
41
42
43
44
45
46
47

> *"Work and play are words used to describe the same thing under differing conditions."* **Mark Twain**

QUESTION?

In what ways can Christians give the devil too much credit? And in what ways too little?

57

1   guaranteed to produce results;

2 ▶ hidden knowledge at last revealed by a teacher of

3   uncommon insight.

4

5 Some current approaches to the world of unclean spirits

6 do not seem to have been present in the life of the

7 church in the New Testament. For example, the

8 concepts that —

9 ▶ we are to 'bind satan' through aggressive prayer,

10   in order that God can be free to work among us.

11 ▶ we can identify, name, talk with or even cast out

12   the principalities and powers over a city or region.

13   Jesus did not use this method with Jerusalem, nor

14   Paul with notorious cities like Ephesus, Corinth

15   and Rome.

16 ▶ we should be scornful, mocking or dismissive

17   towards the forces of evil.

18

19 The first Christians did their business without such odd

20 connections. And so should we.

21

22 **Our weapons**

23 For our fight against spiritual foes, God has provided us

24 with weapons.

25

26 As the body of Christ, together we are to use —

27 ▶ **The Sword of the Spirit** – the Word of God.

28   Rightly handled and proclaimed, the truth about

29   Jesus brings God's revealed will against all the

30   falsehood of the Evil One.

31 ▶ **The proclamation of biblical values** can diminish

32   the destructive, selfish and corrupting influence

33   of the principalities and powers in every aspect of

34   life. This includes issues like business ethics,

35   standards in public life, the care of creation,

36   abortion and euthanasia, Third World

37   development and debt.

38 ▶ **The pursuit of a godly and biblical lifestyle**. This

39   demonstrates the truth and attractiveness of

40   saving faith in Christ. By putting into practice

41   the self-giving and life-enriching love of Christ,

42   together we oppose the selfish and life-destroying

43   guiles of *the evil one*.

44 ▶ **Resisting the enticements of the devil**. In

45   whatever way we may be tempted, simply to

46   refuse to do what we know to be wrong is to

47   undermine his power and authority, causing him

to flee from a confrontation where Jesus is our motivation (1 Peter 5:9).

In our personal daily living

Peter described Satan as a prowling lion, looking for Christians to devour (1 Peter 5:8).

1
2
3
4
5
6
7

QUESTION ?

QUESTION ?

From 1 Peter 5:2–8, find the seven ways given to protect ourselves from Satan, the prowling lion. Write one on each of the seven bars of the cage.

We defend ourselves when we —

▶ serve God willingly (1 Peter 5:2);

▶ are not greedy for reward for our Christian service (1 Peter 5:2);

▶ don't use our authority wrongly in Christian leadership (1 Peter 5:3);

▶ are submissive to those older in the faith (1 Peter 5:5);

▶ are humble towards our fellow Christians (1 Peter 5:5);

37
38
39
40
41
42
43
44
45
46
47

1   ❯ trust God with those things we are anxious about
2   (1 Peter 5:7);
3   ❯ are self-controlled but alert to the danger of sin
4   (1 Peter 5:8).
5
6 **Deliverance**
7 The New Testament speaks of varying degrees of
8 spiritual contamination in which not all demonic
9 possession is equally intense or overwhelming.
10
11 Some Jewish leaders suggested that the success that
12 Jesus had with demons was a kind of spiritual stunt by
13 the prince of darkness himself. Jesus explained that —
14   ❯ his power to deliver was a sign that the Kingdom
15   of God had come and broken out in power on
16   the face of the earth (Matt 12:22ff);
17   ❯ he cast out demons 'by the finger of God'
18   (Luke 11:20).
19
20 Jesus was using language that his Jewish audience would
21 understand clearly. He claimed that the authority he
22 had over the spirit world came direct from the living
23 God. In other words —
24   ❯ Jesus was no mere human exorcist.
25   ❯ Jesus expelled demons with the supreme and
26   irresistible power of God himself.
27
28 Jesus sent out his disciples on mission tours with three
29 tasks —
30   ❯ to preach the good news;
31   ❯ to heal the sick;
32   ❯ to drive out evil or unclean spirits.
33
34 In terms of their role with unclean spirits, Jesus gave the
35 disciples a dynamic of spiritual authority to do the job
36 (Matt 10:1). However, their spiritual authority was
37 derivative.
38
39 The disciples were less effective than Jesus. At least once
40 they could not expel a demon. When Jesus arrived, he
41 was able to provide instantaneous deliverance (Matt
42 17:14–20).
43
44 The followers of Jesus never claimed that they
45 themselves had the spiritual stature to confront and
46 expel unclean spirits. Rather, in the same way that
47 believers were baptised 'in Jesus' name', and prayer was

"All the best work is done the way ants do things—by tiny but untiring and regular additions." **Lafcadio Hearn**

"We are never so ridiculous through what we are as through what we pretend to be." **François, duc de la Rochefoucauld**

to be 'in Jesus' name', demons were to be addressed
only in the name of Jesus (Acts 16:18).

There is more to it than simply using the name of Jesus
as though it were a magic word. Some outside the
church in Ephesus tried to imitate Paul's technique. The
spirit answered with arrogant assertiveness: "Jesus I
know, and I know about Paul, but who are you?"

Then the man with the spirit attacked them with a
superhuman strength, forcing them to run from the
house naked and bleeding (Acts 19:13–16).

A serious business

Jesus has very much greater authority than the demonic
hordes. But they are more powerful than ordinary
human beings who confront them without the
protection of faith in the risen Christ.

In the New Testament, confronting evil spirits is
approached with care .

- Luke, who reports many instances in which
  church leaders cast
  out demons, never
  suggests it is a role
  for every Christian.
- Even the Apostles
  did not look for
  spirits to expel.
  Paul ignored the
  shouts of a
  possessed girl for
  many days. Only
  when he became
  troubled by her
  interruptions did
  he eventually
  command the spirit
  to leave the woman
  (Acts 16:16–18).

1
2
3
4
5
6
7
8
9
10
11
12
13
14
15
16
17
18
19
20
21
22
23
24
25

*"Married and unmarried
women waste a great deal of
time in feeling sorry for each
other."* **Myrtle Reed**

Travel Log

On my visit to the battle zone of Spiritual Warfare

The most interesting thing I saw was ....

....

....

The most surprising thing I saw was ....

....

....

The most important thing I saw was ....

....

....

Because of my visit, in the future I want to try to ....

....

....

FAMILY
– VOYAGE OF DISCOVERY

If only being a Christian were just about Jesus and me. But so many people in his church grieve me. Do they feel the same?

COLOSSIANS 3:12-21

Paul tells the Colossians that they are to select the attitude they express (v12).

Not just individually but corporately they are to clothe themselves with —
- ▶ compassion
- ▶ kindness
- ▶ humility
- ▶ gentleness
- ▶ patience.

Over all this they are to wear the other garment of —
- ▶ love.

Wearing these new garments they are to work out their living relationships together —
- ▶ bearing (putting up) with *each other*
- ▶ forgiving *one another*
- ▶ teaching and admonishing *one another* (v 16).

Paul then works out the detail of these relationships in specific areas of life, linking people together in pairs – husband and wife, father and children, master and slave (v 22). In each case it is important to keep both sides in view to get a balanced picture.

The 'submission' of wives is modelled on the submission of Christ to the Father. So it does not imply any inferiority or lack of value. Such submission —
- ▶ cannot be demanded, but can only be willingly given;
- ▶ represents what is 'fitting' or appropriate within the fellowship of those who are in Christ.

Husbands are to love their **wives**. This is not just affectionately or sexually – but with a love modelled on the love that Christ displayed in the cross (cf Eph 5:25ff). A love that is utterly selfless, wholly servant-like and painfully sacrificial. So there will be none of the bitterness, resentment or anger that come into the meaning of the word 'harsh'.

Children have the duty during their growing-up years to be 'obedient' – which is a stronger and more accurate word than 'submit' – to their parents in every respect.

"Lack of communication does not mean not talking. It means not talking about anything that matters." **Rob Parsons**

HARSH

This comes from a word which means 'sharp or bitter to the taste'. Often described as the effect of bad temper and tyrannical leadership. Cruel husbands were present in the ancient world no less than today.

---

¹²Therefore, as God's chosen people, holy and dearly loved, clothe yourselves with compassion, kindness, humility, gentleness and patience. ¹³Bear with each other and forgive whatever grievances you may have against one another. Forgive as the Lord forgave you. ¹⁴And over all these virtues put on love, which binds them all together in perfect unity.

¹⁵Let the peace of Christ rule in your hearts, since as members of one body you were called to peace. And be thankful. ¹⁶Let the word of Christ dwell in you richly as you teach and admonish one another with all wisdom, and as you sing psalms, hymns and spiritual songs with gratitude in your hearts to God. ¹⁷And whatever you do, whether in word or deed, do it all in the name of the Lord Jesus, giving thanks to God the Father through him.

Rules for Christian Households

¹⁸Wives, submit to your husbands, as is fitting in the Lord.

¹⁹Husbands, love your wives and do not be harsh with them.

²⁰Children, obey your parents in everything, for this pleases the Lord.

²¹Fathers, do not embitter your children, or they will become discouraged.

Of course, Paul addresses these words to a Christian family, where the demands made on children will reflect Christian values and standards.

Fathers (parents) are not to treat their children in a way which causes irritation or embitterment. Perhaps this could be by nagging, derision, or unreasonable punishment.

LIVING IN RELATIONSHIPS

Paul's letter is not to an individual but to a church – and it has to be read against that understanding. He is writing to 'a chosen people' (Col 3:12) not to a chosen person.

This church is made up of people who are to live out their relationships with each other. And these relationships are to be so intimate that they create —
- ▶ the need to put up with each other (v 13)
- ▶ the need to forgive one another (v 13)
- ▶ the opportunity to teach and advise each other (v 16).

Such relationships need to be worked out in this new kingdom through having the right attitudes. These are to be put on – rather like the clothes we choose to wear.

In other words, our new nationality calls for a new national costume. It is a case of new clothes for a new kingdom.

These attitudes can be seen only in relationship to the way we treat one another. Therefore, a church that does not provide opportunities for its members to exist at more than a superficial level of relationships is falling short of God's plan

Paul's instructions are not just so that the Church can get on better – like school rules or the highway code. There is something deeper here.

Jesus said that it would be the quality of love shared between his people that would show them to be his disciples (John 13:34,35)

Writing to the Ephesisians – in a parallel passage – Paul speaks of the Church being a bride for Jesus. A bride

1
2
3
4
5
6
7
8
9
10
11
12
13
14
15
16
17
18
19
20
21
22
23
24
25
26
27
28
29
30
31
32
33
34
35
36
37
38
39
40
41
42
43
44
45
46
47

QUESTION ?

In what ways do the relationships in your church genuinely generate these three needs and opportunities?
What could be done to make this more likely?

QUESTION ?

In what ways is the love between those in your church expressed to that it impacts others?
How could this impact be increased?

"No one ever said on their deathbed, 'I wish I'd spent more time at the office.'"
Rob Parsons

"It is not helpful to help a friend by putting coins in his pocket when he has got holes in his pockets." Douglas Hurd

1 who is radiant, perfect, pure and without blame (Eph
2 5:25–27).
3
4 To understand more of why Paul used this analogy of
5 the bride it is helpful to realise the marriage customs of
6 the time of Jesus.

> The bride is chosen by the bridegroom's father.
> She receives from him a piece of plain cloth from which she makes her wedding dress. It is richly embroidered, reflecting the amount of work she has put into making it.
> The marriage ceremony is *K'ddushim*, which literally means 'being set apart for God.'

15 As the bride, we are part of the daily work of
16 embroidering the cloth – with which we clothe
17 ourselves. We wait for the moment that the bridegroom
18 comes to fetch us.
19

COMMUNICATION

At the heart of any working and meaningful relationship is effective communication. That takes —

> commitment to make it happen;
> time to make it possible.

A lack of effective communication can lead to —

> misunderstanding
> feeling left out and under valued.

Often what people crave is not someone who will talk to them, but someone who will really listen – someone with whom they feel safe enough to share their heart.

Learning to listen

Listening to someone gives them dignity. It says, 'you matter to me – you're important.' The first step is to give the other person your full attention – and to show it.

Listening is a skill that does not always come naturally. But it can be learned with practice.

> Listen with your whole body. Not just your ears, but your voice, your face and the way you position yourself.
> Stop what you are doing and look at the person in the face with care and interest – not a frustrated stare.

"Clothe yourselves with compassion, kindness, humility, gentleness and patience." **Col 3:13**

"To keep a lamp burning, we have to keep putting oil in it." *Mother Theresa*

COLOSSIANS 3 – OVERVIEW

The opening section (vv. 1–4) sets out the theological realities of conversion. The rest of the chapter makes clear the practical implications of conversion —

❖ the things which need to go in vv.5–11;

❖ the things which need to replace them in vv.12–17;

❖ two specific applications in vv.18–25.

Paul had already mentioned their conversion in terms of their baptism (2:12). Now he seems to be making use of the same imagery (cf Rom 6:1–4, where the language is very similar and baptism is specifically mentioned).

Paul reminds them that being a Christian means —

Assuming a new identity. The language is quite startling: "For you died ..." (v.3) and "you have been raised with Christ".

Conversion, says Paul, involves a new creation, an act of resurrection. What is symbolised in baptism is no fiction – they have died with Christ and they have a new life in Christ.

More than that —

❖ in Christ they have been raised with him to the right hand of God;

❖ heaven is now their home;

QUESTION?

List the ways in which you can be sure that someone is listening to you.

their lives are hidden with Christ in God.

Discovering a new dimension. Since this is true, they are to "set their hearts on things above".

This means they are to shape their lives in a new way, a way that —

* reflects their new life and their new home;

* displays a new direction and a new dynamic in their lives.

One day they will openly share the glory of Christ in heaven – but they can start living that reality now.

Commitment to a new way of living. Their old way of life is to go. Instead, they are to increasingly display those Christ-like characteristics which alone are the evidence that they really are citizens of heaven.

Some of the keys to such a transformed life are —

* submission to the shalom of Christ;

* real fellowship;

* a spirit of thanksgiving;

* obedience to the word of God;

* grateful worship;

* Christ-centred living.

Two places where this is to be evident are the family and the workplace.

QUESTION ?

Who do you need to resolve conflict with? How are you going to do it?

---

1 ▶ Use questions to help understand what is being
2 said. And use an indirect approach when asking
3 questions, as direct questioning is often very
4 threatening.
5 ▶ Ask yourself, "Is my listening helping the person
6 to talk, to feel safe enough to be honest, to trust,
7 to feel understood and to make their own
8 decisions."
9 ▶ Give out encouraging signals like a gentle 'I see'
10 or 'yes' or a nod.
11 ▶ Repeat back what you believe you heard.
12 ▶ Listen in a way that listens behind the words to
13 the details and true feelings.
14
15 In our relationships we do not always need a solution to
16 a problem, but we need to feel understood and loved.
17 Good listening undoubtedly improves our relationships
18 and is an effective way of expressing our love and
19 concern.
20

Conflict
21
22 Some married couples claim, 'We've never had an
23 argument in our life', which means that either one of
24 them has completely caved in, or they have the most
25 boring lives in history. The same can be said of
26 churches.
27
28 Much contemporary church life is so sterile and unreal
29 it lacks the opportunity for genuine conflict, or its
30 resolution.
31
32 Conflict is bound to happen in a genuine relationship.
33 The important issue is how we deal with conflict when
34 it comes.
35
36 The golden rules are —
37 ▶ **Never attack the person**. We may let someone
38 know they have done something to upset us.
39 That's fine, as long as we don't use it as a launch
40 pad to a character assassination.
41 ▶ **Stick to the issue**. Many people start off
42 discussing a relatively minor issue that could
43 easily be solved with a small chat. But somehow,
44 loads of other hurts and incidents get dragged
45 into the discussion, which escalates into
46 full-blown battle. At times it may be the other
47 issue that is really the one that needs sorting out

"Unless loving your family is a high priority, you may gain the whole world and lose your children." **Rob Parsons**

"Let us more and more insist on raising funds of love, of kindness, of understanding, of peace. Money will come if we seek first the Kingdom of God—the rest will be given." **Mother Theresa**

1 – rather than the incident that was the last straw.

2 ▶ **Leave the old mortar bombs alone.** Do not drag
3 out things that have already been dealt with.
4 Lock such issues up and toss away the key.

5 ▶ **Learn how to lose an argument.** There is nothing
6 so frustrating as facing someone who is always
7 right. They are brilliant with words, they can
8 summon to mind expert evidence at any time and
9 they cannot face losing an argument.

10

11 People like this may win a lot of battles, but they can
12 lose the war – because the fight is to get closer, not to
13 be right.

14

15 MARRIAGE

16 Paul has some specific instructions for those who are
17 married – in the context of the attitudes that we are to
18 have.

19

20 His instructions on wives submitting (v 15) and
21 husbands loving (v 19) and children obeying (v 20) are
22 in the context of compassion, kindness, humility,
23 gentleness and patience.

24

25 Availability

26 Paul's themes of 'submission' and 'love' demand people
27 having time for each other. In today's world this is
28 harder than ever.

29

30 An anthropologist has estimated that hunter-gatherers
31 spent about five to ten hours a week doing what we
32 now call 'work'. The rest of their time was spent with
33 their family.

34

35 The greatest pressure in marriage often comes from one
36 of the partners being always too busy – at work, in the
37 church or with a hobby. So they simply don't spend
38 enough time together for the relationship to grow.

39

40 The marriage relationship is important enough to plan
41 time together – even put it in the diary – and protect it
42 with your life. When someone comes after that time,
43 tell them you have an appointment with someone who
44 is so important that you could not let them down. And
45 mean it.

46

47 Ways to make this a reality are —

"Spiritually a woman is better off if she cannot be taken for granted."
Germaine Greer

"What has always made the state a hell on earth has been precisely that man has tried to make it his heaven."
Friederich Hölderlin

- A regular meal out – McDonald's if it has to be – with time alone.
- An agenda may sound formal, but it makes sure nothing is missed.
- A night a week without the TV may help.
- Park somewhere – romantic or not.
- Try starting sentences to each other with phrases like, 'What I have been feeling is …', or 'What concerns me is …', or 'I'd like you to know that …', or 'The nicest thing you said or did this past week was …'.

Accepting each other

Trouble can often come when we want our partner to be someone they cannot be.

Most people in a marriage would love to change one or two things about their partner. Sometimes these are justified. If a wife would like her husband to be more careful with his personal hygiene, that is justified.

But —

- comparing our spouse to others, or making impossible demands on them puts them under enormous pressure.
- living with someone who does not accept you the way that you are can be unbearable.

When two people get married, they bring with them a full suitcase of baggage. This is their past, which shapes the way in which they understand the world, their partner and their marriage.

PARENTING

The thing that our children most want from their parents is time. If that is to happen, we need an assault on the unnecessary busyness that we create. This means facing the illusions which rob us of time with our children.

STATS

WORK TODAY

Working hours are getting longer.

Of British male employees —

- ❖ A quarter work more than 48 hours a week.
- ❖ A fifth of all manual workers work more than 50 hours a week.
- ❖ One in 8 managers works over 60 hours a week.
- ❖ Seven out of 10 want to work a 40-hour week – but only three in 10 do.
- ❖ The average 'lunch hour' is now 30 minutes.
- ❖ In the last 10 years, the number of people working 50 hours a week or more has risen over 35 per cent.
- ❖ Today, employers think only two per cent of non-manual staff work 50 hours a week or more. The reality is that 20 per cent do.

At the same time —

- ❖ Full time working women have 14 hours less free time than their male equivalents.

1 **Illusion 1 – 'I have no choice'**
2 Sometimes we can't avoid being busy – we can't always
3 put our families first. But much of our busyness is the
4 direct result of the decisions that we make.
5
6 We may tend to work long hours because everyone at
7 our workplace does and our loyalty to the company can
8 be questioned if we don't. Our busyness may fulfil a
9 need to feel significant; to feel that people need us; to
10 feel that we are important and wanted.
11
12 Sometimes we need to lay down some of our activities
13 and responsibilities to get the time we need to simply
14 be with those who matter.
15
16 **Illusion 2 – 'I'm busy all day'**
17 It seems we have no time for anything. But what are we
18 doing with the time that we do have?
19

Often, we could make better choices and
re-establish our priorities.

It helps to see time as our friend – and
decide whether we really do need to be as
busy as we are. And then take action.

Illusion 3 – 'A slower day is coming'
We often say to ourselves, to our spouses
and to our children, "Things will be
easier/quieter/calmer when …". This
expresses our belief that when the current
32 phase of life is finished we'll have more
33 time for each other, more time for relaxing and being
34 with each other.
35
36 The problem is that —
37 ❯ We create busyness from within ourselves.
38 ❯ No sooner have we finished one project than we
39 are on to the next.
40 ❯ If we are going to make a difference – as mothers
41 and fathers – we are going to have to do it now.
42
43 The decision to be made is practical. It has to do with
44 things like bedtimes, Saturday football matches, stories
45 and hamburgers. It has to do with carving those times
46 out of our busy lives – today.
47

BACKGROUND

MAKING THE MOST OF OUR TIME

❖ See time as something created by God and given to us to enjoy.

❖ List priorities – and stick to them.

❖ Do what needs to be done *now*. And get the most unwelcome task out of the way first.

❖ Work smart. Does it *have* to be done? Can anyone else do it?

❖ Say 'no' – and mean it – recognising that the hours in the day do not expand to take in every new task we commit ourselves to.

QUESTION ?

What could you do to
slow down?
Should you do it?

Unconditional love

The world into which our child is growing up is full of people who will love them when they do well. The world loves a winner. But most of us know ourselves also as losers, and we crave someone who will love us even when we aren't so great.

Much of a child's life is spent in an environment where they are valued providing they achieve. But our children need to hear that we love them and are proud of them at all times.

- The key to a child's heart is to let them know that we love them whatever happens and whatever they do. There is no force on earth more powerful than love that comes without conditions.
- When our children do something well, we can point out that we don't love them to any greater extent – because we couldn't love them any more anyway.

If you want to encourage your children to get things right, praise them when they do. Better than catching them doing something wrong and punishing them is to catch them doing something right and lavish praise and encouragement on them.

Not provoking

If we are not to provoke or embitter our children we must be —

Reasonable

Children need boundaries to feel secure. By setting a boundary, a parent establishes that something is wrong and must not happen.

The time will usually come when that boundary is tested. And then we must hold fast to the boundary that has been set if it is to have any meaning.

Boundaries need to be reasonable and not unduly rigid if they are not to generate resentment and even anger.

Fair

When it comes to discipline, parents are prone to the mistakes of —

- making so many rules that their children are paralysed with a fear of doing something wrong.

"Do not despair: one of the thieves was saved; do not presume: one of the thieves was damned." **St Augustine**

"We think our fathers fools, so wise we grow; Our wiser sons, no doubt will think us so." **Alexander Pope**

1
2
3
4
5
6
7
8
9
10
11
12
13
14
15
16
17
18
19
20
21
22
23
24
25
26
27
28
29
30
31
32
33
34
35
36
37
38
39
40
41
42
43
44
45
46
47

1 ▶ hardly making any rules at all – so that children
2 lack the clear boundaries that they need in order
to feel secure.
▶ Making rules but failing to enforce them – so
that children do not know where they stand.

Don't delegate big issues

In the film *True Lies* the hero cannot control his
teenage daughter. A colleague explains: "You're not
her parents any more. Her parents are Axel Rose
and Madonna. The five minutes you spend with
her cannot compete with that kind of
13 bombardment."
14
15 Modern media uses marketing techniques that have cost
16 millions to develop in order to sell an extraordinary
17 range of ideas and values to our children.   If we want
18 our values to be theirs, it will mean —
19 ▶ taking responsibility for spending the time and
20 effort to teach our children.
21 ▶ Being imaginative in the ways in which we pass
22 on our faith to our children.
23
24 With this in mind, we will do well to remember —
25 ▶ The most important lesson our children will ever
26 receive concerning the Christian faith is how they
27 see you live it from day to day.
28 ▶ Children will learn more from the ways in which
29 God is real and present in the life of those around
30 them than from all the preaching and teaching
31 that they hear.
32
33 **Children and obedience**
34 Children are to obey their Christian parents, Paul says.
35 When he writes in a similar vein to the Ephesians he
36 links this with being obedient to the Ten
37 Commandments (Eph 6:1).
38 ▶ Children are to honour and obey their parents.
39 ▶ They will be rewarded on earth as a result.
40
41 Obedience is more than just carrying out instructions.
42 It involves love, respect and trust.
43
44 Paul is writing in the context of parents expressing the
45 characteristics of the new kingdom in their instruction
46 of their offspring. However, it would never be
47 obedience no matter what the circumstances.

▶ If parents ask a child to contradict God's laws, then the child will obey God (Acts 5:29).

Nor is this a lifelong commitment. When a child becomes an adult, they are no longer under the authority of their parents but responsible for their own decisions.

▶ When children grow up and leave home, they also leave the day-to-day authority that their parents had over them behind. If they get married, the responsibility shifts from parents to partner.

1
2
3
4
5
6
7
8
9
10
11
12
13
14
15
16
17
18
19
20
21
22
23
24

"A man can become so accustomed to the thought of his own faults that he will begin to cherish them as charming little 'personal characteristics'." **Helen Rowland**

TRAVEL LOG

On my voyage of discovery to the Family —

The most interesting thing I saw was ....

....

....

The most surprising thing I saw was ....

....

....

The most important thing I saw was ....

....

....

Because of my visit, in the future I want to try to ....

....

....

FAMILY

THE WORLD OF WORK
– UNEXPLORED TERRITORY

Work dominates life for so many of us. Yet it's a subject the Church largely ignores. Many see 'holy work' as church work. Is this biblical?

COLOSSIANS 3:22–24

Paul's words to slaves do not indicate a thoughtless acceptance of slavery. Nor do they mean that slavery is the model for worker/employer relationships.

What Paul speaks about is the way Christian slaves are to carry out their duties. The principles underlying the behaviour Paul prescribes are relevant to all work situations.

Slaves had no choice but to obey their masters in every respect. But what was important was the way they did it —

- ❯ Not only when supervised – the real test is the quality of work we do which is never seen or checked.
- ❯ Not to win approval or reward from others – currying favour and expecting preferential treatment are unworthy motives for the Christian.

But

- ❯ Conscientiously and singlemindedly;
- ❯ Wholeheartedly;
- ❯ Out of reverence for the Lord – recognising and living out the reality of Christ's lordship in the workplace;
- ❯ In the light of eternity – the future puts our present work into perspective. So we can be confident of a reward if we work well, but equally can expect to be answerable for our failures.

Christians do not work to live, nor do they live to work; they live and work as their service to Christ.

WORK MATTERS

In the nine-to-five or eight-to-eight real world, things have been getting tougher and tougher —

- ❯ longer hours;
- ❯ more part-timers;
- ❯ more short-term contracts;
- ❯ less security;
- ❯ more anxiety;
- ❯ more pressure to be dishonest.

[22]Slaves, obey your earthly masters in everything; and do it, not only when their eye is on you and to win their favour, but with sincerity of heart and reverence for the Lord. [23]Whatever you do, work at it with all your heart, as working for the Lord, not for men, [24]since you know that you will receive an inheritance from the Lord as a reward. It is the Lord Christ you are serving.

QUESTION ?

If work were a journey, would you see it as –
- ❯ an uphill climb?
- ❯ a ramble?
- ❯ an adventure?
- ❯ a bumpy road?

If work were a place to live, would you see it as –
- ❯ a four-star hotel?
- ❯ a tent?
- ❯ a tied cottage?
- ❯ a block of flats?

QUESTION ?

How much, or how little, does this resemble the attitude to work that most people have?
How much is it like your own attitude?

STATS

CHANGE AT WORK
- ❖ The Information Age has replaced the Industrial Age;
- ❖ Over 40,000,000 people worldwide now have an e-mail address;
- ❖ Over the last 10 years, the number of secretaries has declined by a fifth;
- ❖ By the turn of the century, fewer than half of those employed in the industrial world will hold a conventional full time job in an organisation.

²⁵Anyone who does wrong will be repaid for his wrong, and there is no favouritism.

4 Masters, provide your slaves with what is right and fair, because you know that you also have a Master in heaven.

Further Instructions

²Devote yourselves to prayer, being watchful and thankful. ³And pray for us, too, that God may open a door for our message, so that we may proclaim the mystery of Christ, for which I am in chains. ⁴Pray that I may proclaim it clearly, as I should.

QUESTION ?

In what ways does this section express you own understanding of work?
And in what ways does it fill out your picture?

But most churches spend very little time teaching, preaching or praying about the subject of work. In fact, the majority of Christians have received virtually no support for the way they spend well over half of their waking lives.

Research shows that of all Bible-based Christians —
- Half have never heard a sermon on work;
- Three-quarters have never been taught a theology of work or a theology of vocation;
- Only a minority have ever been encouraged to develop a ministry in their workplaces.

As a result, many Christians fail to understand where God fits in during work, where they spend 65 per cent of their time. Or how important their role is.

There are reasons why Christian teaching tends to overlook the whole area of work. These include tendencies to have —
- a false view of what constitutes holy work;
- a false view of Christian ministry;
- a false view of when the church is the Church.

WORK IN THE BEGINNING

The Bible rejects the view that work is a punishment for sin. It was before the Fall that God gave his created beings work to do. However, the Fall made it harder. Work was —
- part of what Adam and Even had to do in the Garden – "work and take care of it" (Gen 2:15);
- made more difficult through their disobedience – "by the sweat of your brow" (Gen 3:19).

This means work can still be a source of satisfaction and joy. After all, the fact that the pain of child-bearing was also increased (Gen 1:16) does not mean that there is no joy in the birth of a child. (See also Ecclesiastes 5:18 and 2:10–11.)

THE WORKER GOD

Work is part of our worship of our loving Creator. Genesis 1 says, "six days he worked". And on the seventh he rested from all the work that he had done.

God is a worker. And work is something he commands us to do as those made in his image.

The factory of the future will have only two employees, a man and a dog. The man will be there to feed the dog. The dog will be there to stop the man from touching the equipment.
Warren Bennis, professor of business administration, University of Southern California.

1 Work is —

2 ▶ not an unfortunate obstacle on the way to the
3   weekend;

4 ▶ not a regrettable barrier to getting to the prayer
5   meeting or getting down to the 'real work of the
6   kingdom';

7 ▶ part of the main action.

8

WORK IS HOLY

10 Paul stresses to the Colossians that their attitude should
11 be in the context of – "Whatever you do … it is the
12 Lord Christ you are serving" (Col 3:24). In other
13 words, our attitude should always be as though what we
14 are doing is for Christ

15

16 So, our relationship with Christ is to have its impact on
17 all that we do, and not just on church work,
18 evangelism, medical care, counselling or teaching.

19

20 We do things to the utmost ability because Jesus makes
21 a difference in our lives. That includes —

22 ▶ Changing a nappy that overflows;

23 ▶ Answering the phone to a client whom we would
24   rather not talk to this side of the fourth
25   millennium;

26 ▶ Reading D H Lawrence because that is the GCSE
27   set text;

28 ▶ Making an arrest, laying a brick, selling a used
29   car, doing a million pound deal, standing up
30   against dishonesty.

31

32 Rightly understood, work is —

33 ▶ Part of the worship we give our Creator;

34 ▶ Part of the way we use the gifts God has given us
35   to their full;

36 ▶ Part of the way we rule over creation (Gen 1:28);

37 ▶ Part of the way we are stewards of the talents and
38   resources God has given us;

39 ▶ Part of the way we, as creatures, rejoice in our
40   createdness;

41 ▶ Part of the way God develops our character,
42   making us reliant on the Holy Spirit to develop
43   the fruit of the Spirit in adversity (Gal 5:22–24).

44

WORK IS VALUABLE

46 Work is significant to God, even if it —

47 ▶ does not have spin-off benefits like evangelistic

and ministry opportunities; 1

- gives little opportunity to earn money to provide 2
  for family and friends; 3
- is making no seeming difference to the quality of 4
  other people's lives. 5

6

Our work may be as a home-maker, car-maker or 7
deal-maker. But — 8

- It is not what we do that determines its value, but 9
  who we do it for. 10
- It is not just how good our work is that 11
  determines its value, but in whose strength it is 12
  done and for whose glory it is offered. 13

14

Work is work whether we are paid for it or not. And 15
just as valuable in God's sight. 16

- Making a bed in a hospital for £6 an hour is 17
  work, so is making a 18
  bed at home for 19
  nothing.
- Working as a chef at
  the Ritz for a
  handsome salary is
  work. So is cooking
  21 meals a week in a
  semi in Newcastle for
  a heartfelt thank you.

QUESTION ?

In what ways does the church convey the impression that the only *real* spiritual work is that done in and for the church?

HOLIER WORK?

Many have an unconscious and false belief that the work of those in so-called 'full-time Christian work' is holier and more important than anything done at home, in a factory or in an office.

From that false belief comes the conclusion that full-time Christian workers are holier than we are.

42
43
44

To put it simply — 44

- we have a false view of what is holy work; 45
- we have a false view of who is a missionary. 46

47

REAL LIFE

CLUMSY FOR CHRIST

Five of us were on a two-day business trip out of town. Surely with all that time God would give me an opportunity to share something with someone. No opportunity came, or at least none that I could see.

The time came to fly home. The client and I decided to work together on the plane. So, briefcase in hand, I negotiated my way into the window seat. As I lifted my case over the seat rest, the lid came open and out tumbled about twenty small orange booklets.

"Oh no," I thought. Twenty copies of a tract called The Four Spiritual Laws scattered over the floor and on the seats in front of me and my client. I felt like a teenager caught with some improper publication. I began to pick them up.

Then the very worst thing that could have happened actually did.

"What are those?" the client asked.

"Errrrr … they're little booklets which explain the main points about Christianity."

I waited for a look of embarrassment. Or perhaps pity. Or discomfort.

"Oh, that's interesting," she said, with a genuinely interested and open expression on her face, "I've been thinking a lot about that recently. Could I have a look?"

You can never tell what's going on in people's lives, can you?

Mark Greene, Thank God it's Monday (SU)

1 As a result —
2 ▶ we pray for ministers and missionaries;
3 ▶ we don't pray for used-car salesmen, managing
4 directors, welders or bank clerks.
5
6 **WORKING TOGETHER**
7 To impact the world of work, we also need to
8 understand the nature and role of the church. Most
9 people, however, feel they go to work alone.
10
11 This is because, we fail to understand that we are still
12 church – still a community – when we are out there,
13 scattered like so many grains of salt in the world.
14
15 The Church is always the Church —
16 ▶ when we meet together for worship and teaching;
17 ▶ when we work out our relationship together in
18 the local community – showing people by the
19 way we love one another that we are Jesus'
20 disciples (John 13:35);
21 ▶ when we are scattered like salt to work out our
22 faithfulness to Christ in the world at large.
23
24 When *at work* we should be experiencing all the help
25 that is available from God's word, God's spirit and
26 God's people.
27
28 Most pastors/teachers have their eyes focused almost
29 exclusively on the neighbourhood of the church
30 building, rather than the neighbourhoods of those who make up the Church family. It is not hard to see how short sighted this is.

MISSIONARY WORKERS
Stephen used to be an accountant. Now he's a missionary in Paris. His letters include requests to pray for people by name.

Kevin is a housegroup leader – seen by the other members most Tuesday evenings and regularly at church. They do not know the name of anyone he works

QUESTION ?

Why do we tend only to pray for ministers and missionaries? What does this say about our view of work outside of the church? What can we do about it?

with. And have never prayed for them.

This is because Stephen is a missionary and Kevin isn't. Or so we think. But who has relationships with non-Christians? Kevin in the maelstrom of the National Health Service? Or Stephen working from a missionary office in Paris?

Who do those outside the church see struggling with anger and frustration; success and failure; limited resources and sexual temptation; gossip and the challenge to tell the truth; the threat and sometimes reality of redundancy?

Where is someone more likely to see the difference that Jesus makes to someone's life? In Kevin's situation or Stephen's?

The answers are obvious. Yet there is little training about how we can make an impact in our workplaces. And most evangelistic enterprise is centred around local neighbourhoods and getting people into the church building, not about helping work out the implications of being a citizen of the Kingdom of Heaven where we are.

Who is the minister anyway?

Because we have not taken seriously what pastors/teachers are called to do, we have been getting the issues of ministry, work and evangelism wrong.

Ephesians 4:11–12 reads:
"It was he (Jesus) who gave some to be apostles, some to be prophets, some to be evangelists, and some to be pastors and teachers, **to prepare God's people** for works of service, so that the body of Christ may be built up … ."

Here Paul is saying that —
- The job of a pastor and teacher includes that of equipping the people of God for *their* ministry.
- The pastor/teacher is to resource us for *our* ministry, rather than simply to equip us as volunteers in theirs.

This is a role that pastors/teachers are quite able

1
2
3
4
5
6
7
8
9
10
11
12
13
14
15
16
17
18
19
20
21
22
23
24
25
26
27

REAL LIFE

IN THE BAR

We are in a bar having a farewell drink for one of the team. I'm talking to Susan. We've been working together for about a year, and we get round to C.S. Lewis. Barbara (or at least that's what we'll call her) is with us. She's Jewish, bright and fun.

"Is that the same C.S. Lewis who wrote the Narnia Chronicles?"

"Yes."

"I love those books. He's my hero. I didn't know he was a Christian."

"Oh, yes, and there's Christian allegory in the books. Aslan is Jesus…"

"Yeah, but Aslan comes back to life…"

God at work. The Christian at work.

Mark Greene, Thank God it's Monday (SU)

1 to do – if they see its importance, and if we give them
2 the opportunity.
3
4 Pastors/teachers are also quite able to understand the
5 challenges faced by those who
are in the regular work force.

This is because —

▶ Many pastors once had a life
in the 'normal' world and can
relate to what this means.

▶ Pastors have been trained to
listen, trained to look into
God's all-sufficient word and
to come back with answers to
the tough questions.

Those who are pastors and
teachers in the church are well
able to teach us about work and
vocation; ambition and
promotion; handling the
disappointments of being passed
over; success and failure;
attitudes to bosses; honesty and
truth-telling; leisure.

In doing so,
they have
resources of

29
30 their knowledge of the Bible to teach
31 us about courageous midwives (Ex
32 1:15–20); administrator Daniel;
33 Prime Minister Joseph (Gen 39ff);
34 Naaman's unnamed servant girl (2
35 Kings 5); merchant Lydia (Acts
36 16:13–15 and 40).
37
38 They can also help us apply the
39 framework of the Bible to the
40 unethical practices that abound in
41 some contemporary workplaces, like
42 —
43 ▶ sexism;
44 ▶ racism;
45 ▶ bullying;
46 ▶ abuse of suppliers …
47

BACKGROUND

SIX LEVELS OF WITNESS AT WORK

1 **The witness of Christ in you**
He's in us and, however flawed we are, he is working
(2 Cor 5:17).

2 **The witness of your work**
Not simply how good it is, but in whose strength it is
produced and for whose glory.

3 **The witness of a biblical perspective on personal
issues**
Our coworkers are facing alll kinds of issues at home
and at work – issues that we can offer biblical wisdom
about without necessarily even mentioning the Bible.

4 **The witness of a biblical perspective on general issues**
You're in the canteen or chatting over a cup of coffee.
What are people talking about? Last night's TV show?
This morning's headlines? How can we bring biblical
wisdom to bear on the issues raised in the culture
around us?

5 **The witness of a biblical perspective on work/business
issues**
Are there practises in your workplace that need to be
challenged or affirmed? There may be an opportunity
or a need for you to bring biblical perspective to bear
on issues such as appraisals, pay, racism, sexism,
honesty, etc. But it takes time, and probably talking to
others, to work on the solutions.

6 **Sharing the gospel**
We can prepare the soil through the way we work and
relate to others, but people need to hear the Good
News. Pray for your coworkers, for opportunities to
share and for the courage to take them when they arise.

TRAVEL LOG

**During my visit to the unexplored territory
of the World of Work —**

The most interesting thing I saw was ....

....

....

The most surprising thing I saw was ....

....

....

The most important thing I saw was....................................

....

....

Because of my visit, in the future I want to try to ....

....

....

EVANGELISM
– TRAVELLERS TALES

So far as evangelism is concerned, those inside the church and those outside it are in complete agreement: both hate it.
But there is hope.

COLOSSIANS 4:5–6

These verses provide a splendid mini-manual on sharing our faith with those as yet 'outside'. It is not only Paul – and leaders like him – who are called to share the good news (vv.2–3). All Christians are witnesses – able to speak of what they know to be true – to God's love in Jesus.

Paul gives us five pointers.

Be wise – This implies a thoughtful and prayerful approach to others. It involves seeking to know in a practical, down-to-earth way what God wants us to do or say in a particular situation. We are to be bold and open in sharing the gospel. But tact and sensitivity are needed so as not to give offence.

Be vigilant – Be on the lookout for opportunities to share the good news. When they come, make the most of them. Grasp them. Snap them up. Don't let any opportunity escape.

Be gracious – especially in the way we speak to others, whether in preaching or in conversation. Our words should reflect, and our manner underline, the gracious love of the Father we represent.

Be interesting – Don't be bland, but "seasoned with salt". Not dull or boring; rather – while remaining winsome and wholesome – be witty, arresting, stimulating.

Be personal – Treat each person individually, beginning where they are, listening to what they say, and giving them your whole attention.

OUR JERUSALEM

Without there having been obedience to the directions of Jesus, the Colossian church would never have come into existence. The challenge we face is how we can be equally obedient and so see the church grow where we are.

The people of God have glorious beliefs and a magnificent story to tell. But —

▶ we must learn how to relate to those round about

MAKE THE MOST

A phrase from the market place. "Snap up that bargain. Don't miss that special offer. Buy before someone else gets in before you." All these phrases convey something of the meaning of this phrase in Colossians 4:5.

---

[5] Be wise in the way you act toward outsiders; make the most of every opportunity. [6] Let your conversation be always full of grace, seasoned with salt, so that you may know how to answer everyone.

Final Greetings

[7] Tychicus will tell you all the news about me. He is a dear brother, a faithful minister and fellow servant in the Lord. [8] I am sending him to you for the express purpose that you may know about our[13] circumstances and that he may encourage your hearts. [9] He is coming with Onesimus, our faithful and dear brother, who is one of you. They will tell you everything that is happening here.

[10] My fellow prisoner Aristarchus sends you his greetings, as does Mark, the cousin of Barnabas. (You have received instructions about him; if he comes to you, welcome him.) [11] Jesus, who is called Justus, also sends greetings. These are the only Jews among my fellow workers for the kingdom of God, and they have proved a comfort to me. [12] Epaphras, who is one of you and a servant of Christ Jesus, sends greetings. He is always wrestling in prayer for you, that you may stand firm in all the will of God, mature and fully assured. [13] I vouch for him that he is working hard for you and

[13] 8 Some manuscripts *that he may know about your*

for those at Laodicea and Hierapolis. ¹⁴Our dear friend Luke, the doctor, and Demas send greetings. ¹⁵Give my greetings to the brothers at Laodicea, and to Nympha and the church in her house.

¹⁶After this letter has been read to you, see that it is also read in the church of the Laodiceans and that you in turn read the letter from Laodicea.

us at the level of our common humanity;

▶ we need to find ways to wrap our orderly framework of belief round the story of life.

Douglas Coupland, a contemporary writer with no church links, concludes his book *Life After God* with these poignant words of challenge: "My secret is that I need God – that I am sick and can no longer make it alone. I need God to help me give because I no longer seem capable of giving; to help me be kind, as I no longer seem capable of kindness; to help me love, as I seem beyond being able to love."

Why is he not looking to the church to find God? Because we have become such an inward-looking sub-culture that we cannot communicate with those outside our circle

BE WISE
Be wise about today's culture
The attitudes and understanding of the people around us are very different to those of the people who surrounded the Christians in Colossae. In particular, theirs was a 'pre-Christian' culture. The gospel had yet to penetrate their society.

In contrast, the gospel has already penetrated our society – many of whom have now moved on and left it behind.

The Colossians were about to build the church. In our society the building is largely derelict – but still exerts some residual influence.

A jargon word for our culture is that it is *post-Christian*.
▶ There is still an awareness and 'tradition' of Christian belief and values.
▶ There is a growing ignorance of the Bible and the truth about Jesus.
▶ A recent MORI poll showed almost three-fifths of 18–24 year olds have no idea what event took place on Good Friday.
▶ Fifty years ago, half the population believed in an afterlife. Today, only two-fifths believe.
▶ Fifty years ago, one-fifth of the population did not believe in an afterlife. Today, two-fifths do not believe.

"He who looks only at heaven may easily break his nose on earth." **Czech proverb**

QUESTION ?

What advantages and opportunities does the fact that we are a post-Christian nation give us?
And what disadvantages?

1
2
3
4
5
6
7
8
9
10
11
12
13
14
15
16
17
18
19
20
21
22
23
24
25
26
27
28
29
30
31
32
33
34
35
36
37
38
39
40
41
42
43
44
45
46
47

1 ❱ Disbelief in God has risen from one in ten, to
2 one in four.
3 ❱ Belief in a personal (Christian) God has shrunk
4 to 30 per cent from 45 per cent.
5 ❱ Many who have no knowledge of a personal god
6 still see themselves as Christians and use the
7 rights of passage offered by the church.
8
9 To use more jargon, our culture is also *post-modern*.
10 This is a way of describing the passing of the era of
11 modernity – with its certainties about life having
12 meaning, purpose and a 'big picture'.
13
14 Our post-modern era is one where people have begun
15 to realise that the optimistic hopes, dreams and
16 promises of modernism have not been fulfilled.
17 Post-modernism says that —
18 ❱ There is no one complete answer – to anything.
19 ❱ There are no certainties – other than that there
20 are no certainties..
21 ❱ There is no great theme and meaning to life.
22 ❱ Truth is only to be known through experience.
23 ❱ What is true for one person need not be true for
24 others – and they should never insist that it is.
25
26 Our post-modern culture presents people with a choice
27 of views about what is true and important as the basis
28 for life. From these they are to pick and mix – with
29 Christianity as just one alternative on the list.
30
31 At the same time as Christianity has been put on the
32 shelf, a wide range of other world views has been
33 developed in our culture, or been imported from other
34 cultures. Or blended from the two. These include —
35 ❱ Secular humanism;
36 ❱ Eastern mysticism;
37 ❱ Scientific materialism;
38 ❱ Wicca paganism.
39
40 Our post-Christian, post-modern culture has become
41 increasingly fragmented. Sociologists talk of
42 'neo-tribalism' – the idea that our modern society is
43 made up of lots of small sub-cultures all with their own
44 beliefs and values, likes and dislikes. These sub-cultures
45 can be as varied as —
46 ❱ Travellers
47 ❱ Freemasons

"I imagine that one of the reasons people cling to their hates so stubbornly is because they sense, once hate is gone, that they will be forced to deal with pain." **James Baldwin**

"Let none turn over books, or roam the stars in quest of God, who sees him not in man." **Johann Kaspar Lavater**

COLOSSIANS 4 – OVERVIEW

The closing sections of Paul's letters are often made up of a host of short comments and brief greetings. These can seem relatively unimportant compared with what has appeared earlier. But they repay careful study.

In v.1 "masters" are reminded that they too are accountable to a Master – who provides them with a pattern to follow in the exercise of their own lordship over others.

As in some of his other letters, Paul emphasises the importance of prayer in his concluding comments —

❖ Prayer should be of prime importance in the life of the Colossians (c.2);

❖ The role of prayer was seen in the fine example of their fellow-countryman, Epaphras (v.12);

❖ Through prayer they can actively share in Paul's ministry – asking for opportunity and clarity in sharing the gospel (vv.3–4).

The Colossians themselves were encouraged to seize every opportunity – wisely

- ▶ Suburban commuters
- ▶ Neo-Nazis
- ▶ Club-goers
- ▶ Football hooligans
- ▶ Trainspotters
- ▶ Prisoners
- ▶ Old people in homes
- ▶ Career women
- ▶ Computer geeks
- ▶ Bikers.

This brings the need to adopt many different evangelism strategies in order to relate to different groups of people.

Many churches have discovered that putting on events or programmes designed to reach everybody, means they end up reaching nobody. So they ask God to help them decide which sub-cultures they should try to reach – and then plan activities specifically for them.

Community

There is a new emphasis both politically and in society on restoring a sense of community life. God, the Holy Trinity, is community, and in that community of love we find our identity.

Jesus' command has never been more relevant: "Love one another as I have loved you. By this everyone will know that you are my disciples" (John 13:34,35).

This is not a reference to how we are to behave when together in meetings – but how to live together within the community. The bond of our relationships in everyday life should be such that it demonstrates the supernatural presence of Jesus.

The most powerful witness to the truth about Jesus is the fact that we can be seen to love one another. If we cannot find ways to do that, then we might as well pack up.

Making the Best of Things

We have tried all kinds of techniques and reforms in the church in the past 50 years, and seen a steady decline in the West.

and winsomely – to make the good news known (vv.5–6).

All Christians have a part to play in mission. The rest of the chapter shows just how much of a team effort it is, as Paul mentions numerous people who have tasks to perform. Of the men trained by Paul —

- ❖ some are well known to us;
- ❖ others are mentioned only here;
- ❖ some have failed in the past but are now to be encouraged (v.10);
- ❖ others are helpful now but are not immune from failure in the future (v.14).

We see Paul here as a real person (v.6) who very much needs and appreciates human companionship (v.11). And who, in the midst of his own loneliness and frailty, is constantly thinking of others and has a message for each of them.

His final message, to Archippus in v.17 – to complete the work he had received from the Lord – is clearly a word to all God's people in all times and places. Including us.

"Generation X has come into young adult maturity in a cultural and moral 'whirlwind of barbarism'. We believe that the characteristics for which Generation X has received such bad press are the very qualities that will render them most effective as pioneers of a revitalised Christian faith.
"Their pragmatism and scepticism, their sharp-eyed assessments of life, and above all their search for community and personal relationships are exactly what the emerging era requires."
William Mahedy and Janet Bernardi, *A Generation Alone: Xers Making a Place in the World,* **Downers Grove, Ill: IVP, 1994.**

1 Perhaps God is forcing upon us, through our culture,
2 the opportunity to disciple a generation who are 'open'
3 but do not know where to turn.
4
5 Here is a new opportunity and a new moment.
6
7 **"MAKE THE MOST OF EVERY OPPORTUNITY"**
8 **God makes the opportunities, we just make the**
9 **most of them.**
10 There is no need to engineer opportunities to tell those
11 we are in contact with about Jesus. If we have been
12 praying and preparing ourselves for such opportunities,
13 God will provide them. We just have to make the most
14 of them.
15
16 **Some problems are really opportunities!**
17 Today, most people are not interested in hearing about
18 Jesus. That means starting much further back.
19
20 For example, there is usually little point in beginning to
21 talk about Jesus' death on the cross to someone who
22 does not yet understand that God exists and that he
23 loves them.
24
25 This may seem like a great problem – because the cross
26 is the centre of our faith and we want to tell people
27 about it. But that problem is also a great opportunity.
28
29 The message of the cross is offensive to many people.
30 But the message that God exists and that he loves them
31 is not offensive. It actually opens doors. This does not
32 mean watering down the message – but presenting the
33 part of the gospel message that is an appropriate
34 starting point for today's culture.
35
36 Many Christians who are taking this approach are
37 finding previously-undreamed-of openings for the
38 gospel – including opportunities to speak in the media,
39 in schools and at community events.
40
41 This has also contributed to change in another way —
42 ▶ Once the church was right at the centre of the
43 community.
44 ▶ More recently, Christians have been rejected and
45 marginalised – or have marginalised themselves.
46 ▶ Now, many churches are finding themselves with
47 opportunities to be back in the centre of the

QUESTION ?

What opportunities could you take to express the truth about Jesus in a relevant way?
What stops you?

community once more.

"LET YOUR CONVERSATION ..."
Evangelism is not just about preaching

Throughout the history of the church, people have become Christians when they have heard the gospel presented through preaching. But this is not the only way in which they have come to faith. Nor is it necessarily the most productive.

Most evangelism flows from natural conversation – and not always when dealing with deep theological subjects. Indeed —

▶ Most evangelism takes place in the context of real life – in the office, over meals, either side of a garden fence, in a student bar, and so on.
▶ Evangelism that is true to the Bible allows people to ask questions and work through their doubts.

The conversational approach is at the heart of the way the first Christians spread their message —

▶ Philip listened to the Ethiopian's question. That was how he was able to help him (Acts 6).
▶ Paul reasoned and debated with people in the synagogues and in the market-places (Acts 13:16ff, 43,44; Acts 14:1; Acts 16:13,14; Acts 17:2, 17).
▶ Paul also brought his tentmaking business to town and chatted to his customers.

The conversational approach is also the way Jesus dealt with individuals. Jesus taught the crowds through public speaking, and evangelised individuals through conversation. For example —

▶ The woman at the well (John 4:1–26);
▶ Nicodemus (John 3:1–21).

Because this approach is biblical, it is also successful. For example —

▶ The success of the Alpha courses is partly due to enquirers being given plenty of opportunity to ask questions.
▶ Some of the most effective evangelistic activities include talk-back sessions – providing opportunities for people to raise questions and objections.

1
2
3
4
5
6
7
8
9
10
11
12
13
14
15
16
17
18
19
20
21
22
23
24
25
26
27
28
29
30
31
32
33
34
35
36
37
38
39
40
41
42
43
44
45
46
47

QUESTION ?

What more could you do to listen to the questions of others, including those that they do not express in words?

1 Conversation is the very opposite of confrontation. And
2 this is a big lesson for the church to learn. For too long
3 we have expressed our desire for people to come into
4 the Kingdom of Heaven through *in-your-face*
5 arguments. In contrast, when Jesus wanted to help
6 honest seekers learn more, he fell in step with them,
7 joining them on their journey (Luke 13:24).
8
9 The over-emphasis on confrontation may be partly due
10 to wrong understanding of the process that most people
11 pass through on their journey towards personal belief.
12 ❱ We can wrongly imagine that people hear the
13   gospel, then believe, and then set about looking
14   for fellowship.
15 ❱ In reality, people tend to have contact with
16   Christians, join the fellowship and later come to a
17   personal faith.
18
19 This means that some of our conversation is likely to be
20 in the context of an involvement with church life.
21 Where they have come, in some way, to see 'your
22 church' as 'their church'.
23
24 So if the life of our church is so structured that it only
25 has a place for those who are 'saved and sanctified', we
26 are in trouble. And this is no new idea. This was much
27 the way it seemed to be in the churches of the New
28 Testament, judging from the kind of errors and
29 behaviour that Paul needed to address, and the
30 qualifications for leadership that he had to impose.
31
32 **"… BE FULL OF GRACE …"**
33 **It's not just what you say – it's the way you say it**
34 Evangelism is about much more than the words that we
35 use. It is about being a certain person and living in a
36 certain way.
37 ❱ Sometimes our lives can speak so loudly that
38   people cannot hear the words we say.
39
40 A life that shows the grace of which Paul speaks will be
41 marked by —
42 ❱ loving, caring and compassionate actions –
43   energised by the love of God in our hearts;
44 ❱ the absence of any desire to win a battle or prove
45   ourselves right;
46 ❱ a genuine concern for the wellbeing – present and
47   future – of those with whom we are sharing the

QUESTION ?

What more can you and your church do to 'walk with people on their journey' rather than confront them?

good news;

▶ a willingness to listen and to show respect for the other person.

We are almost certain to inflict boredom if we —

▶ talk about the church rather than Jesus;
▶ answer questions that people are not asking;
▶ use language and concepts that people do not easily understand;
▶ fail to tell stories and paint pictures in people's minds. We should be using words that can be drawn – like *road*, *sheep*, *light*, *son* and *party*. Rather than words that can't be drawn – like *salvation*, *hope*, *sin*, *injustice* and *redemption*;
▶ talk about our world rather than theirs.

So there is no reason for the good news ever to appear boring and irrelevant.

1
2
3
4
5
6
7
8
9
10
11
12
13
14
15
16
17
18
19
20

"… SEASONED WITH SALT …"
The gospel has flavour

There is no-one more exciting than Jesus. How many other people can calm a storm, walk on water or rise from the dead? And who else offers to come and live inside us, transforming our lives supernaturally?

Recent research indicates that —

▶ where parents talk mainly about 'church', their children usually do not become Christians;
▶ where parents talk mainly about 'Jesus', the children usually do become Christians.

"… SO THAT YOU MAY KNOW HOW TO ANSWER …"
Having 'a reason for our faith' is as important as it always was.

In our post-Christian, post-modern culture, people no

QUESTION ?

What 'pictures' and stories have helped you to understand the good news about Jesus?

BACKGROUND

Isn't Christianity just a psychological crutch?

Can we dismiss someone's faith by implying that in some way they *need* to believe it and therefore do. If so, a Christian could also retort that an atheist is someone who doesn't want to bother about obeying God's commands, so – hey presto – there is no God.

To claim that Christian experience is *just* psychological ignores the fact that it involves psychological aspects of our lives – our minds, emotions and wills. For example, a physicist could describe cricket in terms of velocity, mass, density and distance. But he knows that cricket is not just a series of principles in physics. There are other dimensions – the rules of the game, winning and competing, and so on.

Christian conversion is like this. It is psychological, but when you have said this you have only commented on one small aspect of the whole experience.

No!

So could Christianity be a crutch – like alcohol or drugs? Something to help the weak through tough situations – as if Christians were basically failures as people and needed something to help them get by. So if Christianity were false, it would be a useless crutch. At least alcohol works, even if only for a short time. But if Christianity *is* true, it is a cure not a crutch. 'Is Christianity *true*?' is the vital question. American writer and speaker Joni Eareckson-Tada became a quadriplegic after a diving accident when she was 17. Yet she has said, 'I believe in Jesus not because it is easy but because it is true.'

Adapted from Stephen Gaukroger, It Makes Sense, *Scripture Union*

1 longer start with the same questions posed by earlier
2 generations. Questions like —
3 ◗ Is Jesus really unique?
4 ◗ Are the Gospels reliable?
5
6 These questions come later, after they have been
7 provoked to think seriously about the Christian gospel.

The things that are likely to stir their interest are —

◗ observing the lives of Christians that are positively different;

◗ recognising they have a spiritual dimension to their life that needs to be fed.

Then the time will come when we need to know how to answer the questions that this will generate.

BACKGROUND

TO FIND OUT MORE

Books that help answer the questions people ask about the Christian faith include —

- ❖ John Stott, *Basic Christianity*, IVP
- ❖ C.S. Lewis, *Mere Christianity*, Found
- ❖ Josh McDowell, *Evidence that Demands a Verdict*, *Christianity: A Ready Defence*, *Answers to Tough Questions*, Scripture Press
- ❖ Don Stewart, *Reasons Why We Should Consider Christianity*, Scripture Press
- ❖ Nicky Gumbel, *Questions of Life*, *Searching Issues*, *Why Jesus?*, Kingsway
- ❖ Ravi Zacharias, *Can Man Live Without God?*, Word
- ❖ Jock Stein and Howard Taylor, *In Christ All Things Hold Together*, Fount
- ❖ James Jones, *Why do People Suffer?*, Lion
- ❖ John Drane, *The Bible: Fact or Fantasy?*, Lion
- ❖ John Houghton, *The Search for God: Can Science Help?*, Lion
- ❖ Michael Poole, *A Guide to Science and Belief*, Lion
- ❖ Stephen Gaukroger, *It Makes Sense*, Scripture Union

26
27
28 **Which questions will we be asked?**
29 Whether in conversational evangelism or in
30 seeker-friendly events featuring talk-back opportunities,
31 you can be sure that these ten questions will crop up
32 regularly:
33   1.   If God is so good, why is there so much
34   suffering?
35   2.   Why does God let bad people get away with
36   it?
37   3.   Hasn't science disproved Christianity?
38   4.   What about those who've never heard the
39   gospel?
40   5.   How can other religions be wrong?
41   6.   How can miracles be possible?
42   7.   Isn't the Bible full of errors/why believe the
43   Bible?
44   8.   Isn't faith just psychological?
45   9.   How can a God of love send anyone to hell?
46   10.   What is it about your life that is so different?
47

1
2
3
4
5
6
7
8
9
10
11
12
13
14
15
16
17
18
19
20
21
22
23

TRAVEL LOG

EVANGELISM

On my travels to Evangelism

The most interesting thing I saw was ....

....

....

The most surprising thing I saw was ....

....

....

The most important thing I saw was.......................................

....

....

Because of my visit, in the future I want to try to ....

....

....

46
47

PRESSING ON

— THE FINAL FRONTIER

Starting can be hard. But finishing with a flourish can be tougher. Yet that is what we are called to do.

 PRESSING ON

EVANGELISM  FALSE TEACHING

SALVATION
UNLIMITED ENTRY—UNLIMI
UNLIMITED ENTRY—UNLIMI

COLOSSIANS 4:17

"Never give in! Never give in! Never, never, never. Never — in anything great or small, large or petty — never give in except to convictions of honour and good sense." **Winston S.Churchill**

COLOSSIANS 4:17

Paul's final message is a personal one to Archippus – someone about whom we know very little. He is also mentioned in Paul's letter to Philemon.

Archippus —

- is referred to in Philemon 2 as 'our fellow soldier', a way of describing someone who shares in the service of the gospel such as Epaphroditus (Phil 2:25) and Timothy (2 Tim 2:3);
- could possibly have been Philemon's son, or helping to rehabilitate his runaway slave Onesimus;
- may have been a deacon, in charge of a collection, or most likely involved in preaching and teaching.

Whatever his role and background, the important thing is Paul's message to him. Archippus was told not to give up. He was to stick at it and see his task through to the end. Whether it was going well or whether he was tired and discouraged, he was to keep going and finish the job.

Someone was once described as 'great at running the 95-yard dash'. That is a distinction nobody needs. It's the last five yards that make the first 95 worthwhile.

FINISHING WELL

Paul's word of encouragement and instruction to Archippus – and to us – is to finish what he had started.

In his letters, Paul uses the word *perseverance* or *keeping on* to express the same thought. (See Eph 6:18, where he uses it to emphasise persistance in prayer.)

The idea of perseverance, steadfastness, patience and persistence is confirmed by the use of an original verb that means to attend constantly, to adhere firmly or hold on to something as we endeavour to finish the task.

The same word is used in —

- Mark 3:9 to describe a skiff quietly waiting to carry Jesus away from a surging crowd;

[17]Tell Archippus: "See to it that you complete the work you have received in the

Lord."

[18]I, Paul, write this greeting in my own hand. Remember my chains. Grace be with you.

▶ Acts 10:7 of the soldiers in Cornelius' bodyguard who were continuously serving him.

In its spiritual application, this verb always has to do with continuing in the Christian way, particularly in relation to prayer. See Acts 1:14, 2:42,46, 6:4, Rom 12:12 and Col 4:2.

WORK TO BE DONE

In the church, everyone has a role to play and a job to do. Before facing the issue of perseverance, we need to find our place and get a role to persevere with.

Church is not about what we can get out, it's about what we can put in. It's firstly about giving, not receiving. And God equips us with extra ability – spiritual gifts – to play our part.

When Paul writes about spiritual gifts (1 Cor 12), he describes the church as the body of Christ. And no part of the body can do without the others, he says —

▶ "The eye cannot say to the hand, 'I don't need you'." (1 Cor 12:21)

You are an important part of the body of Christ, and it will not work properly without you.

FINISH WHAT YOU START

The need to see things through to the end is good advice for everything in life. But Paul here is dealing with work for God.

He may well have had in mind —

The teaching of Jesus

▶ Facing would-be followers who want to attend to other priorities first, Jesus told them: "No-one who puts his hand to the plough and looks back is fit for service in the Kingdom of Heaven" (Luke 9:62);

▶ When talking to his disciples, Jesus told them to be ready for service – watchful and working at the task given them by their master (Luke 12:35–46);

1
2
3
4
5
6
7
8
9
10
11
12
13
14

QUESTION ?

What specific gifts and abilities to serve God –
▶ have you seen in others?
▶ have you seen in yourself?

BACKGROUND

GIFTS OF THE HOLY SPIRIT

The range of supernatural gifts that God gives to those who are in his church is wide reaching. The following list draws on those that Paul mentions in three of his letters. Rom 12:6–8; 1 Cor 12:8–10; Eph 4:11–12

The 'General' Gifts

❖ Service
❖ Helping
❖ Intercession
❖ Motivation
❖ Mercy
❖ Hospitality
❖ Encouragement
❖ Giving
❖ Celibacy
❖ Martyrdom

The 'Ministry' Gifts

❖ Apostle
❖ Missionary
❖ Pastor
❖ Leadership
❖ Administration
❖ Evangelism
❖ Teacher
❖ Exorcism

The 'Extraordinary' Gifts

– of revelation

❖ Discerning of spirits
❖ Word of knowledge
❖ Word of wisdom

– of activity

❖ Healing
❖ Miracles
❖ Faith

–of communication

❖ Tongues
❖ Interpretation
❖ Prophecy

1 ▶ Jesus also taught his disciples specifically about
2 not giving up when praying, using the parable of
3 the persistent widow (Luke 18:1–8).
4

5 **The example of Jesus**
6 ▶ Jesus spoke of "the work that the Father has given
7 me to finish, and which I am doing" (John 5:36);
8 ▶ Jesus knew that the goal of his work was the
9 cross. He progressed firmly towards it and
10 allowed nothing to alter his resolute approach
11 (Luke 9:51);
12 ▶ At the moment before he died on the cross, he
13 was able to speak the last words: "It is finished".
14 He had completed the task given to him by his
15 Father.
16

17 **Paul's own teaching**
18 ▶ Paul understood the 'finish-what-you-start'
19 principle and taught it to others. Writing to the
20 Christians at Philippi he put the emphasis on
21 God doing the work: "… that he who began a
22 good work in you will carry it on to completion
23 until the day of Christ Jesus" (Phil 1:6);
24 ▶ Paul reminded the Corinthians in 2 Cor 8:10,11
25 that they should complete the work they began –
26 in giving money for the impoverished Jerusalem
27 church.
28

29 **Paul's own example**
30 Perseverance has been well described as 'courage
31 stretched out'. Certainly Paul's perseverance in doing
32 God's work was courageous in physical, mental and
33 spiritual terms —
34 ▶ He was imprisoned, stoned, beaten, shipwrecked
35 and more (2 Cor 11:23–27);
36 ▶ He went through conflict with his fellow apostles
37 and Christian companions (Gal 2:11ff, Acts
38 15:36–40);
39 ▶ He felt a constant pressure of concern for the
40 churches he had planted and nurtured (2 Cor
41 11:28,29).
42

43 Although God sometimes rescues his people from
44 difficult or painful circumstances, he more often calls us
45 to a courageous and enduring faithfulness in the midst
46 of trials. So perseverance is not only enduring situations
47 of suffering, but overcoming them with obedience,

"Great works are performed not by strength but by perseverance." **Samuel Johnson**

hope and joy

Let's look at two examples from the Old Testament.

Joshua
"Your entire army is to march around the city once a day for six days" (Josh 6:1–20).

As a member of Joshua's army, would you have felt like giving up – or at least questioning the leadership – if after six full days nothing had happened?

Perseverance is continuing to obey God even when his command doesn't make sense or seem to be productive from our human perspective.

Nehemiah
"I realised that God had not spoken to him ..." (Neh 6:1–15).

The Christian's task and the perseverance to finish the task are rooted in God's call.

The job of rebuilding the broken walls of Jerusalem was too big. Then to make sure it didn't get done, the scoffers tried to intimidate the people involved. But the walls were rebuilt anyway – in a remarkable 52 days.

The perseverance of Nehemiah and the people had paid off. God's men and women, joined together for special tasks, can solve huge problems and accomplish great goals if they are doing what God wants them to do. And seeing it through to completion.

OUR WORK SHOULD BE HIS WORK
Paul's instruction is to complete the work "received in the Lord" (Col 4:17). Much that is done in the name of the Lord is our work rather than his.

QUESTION ?

In what ways have you benefited from the encouragement of others?
In what ways have you been an encourager of others?

BACKGROUND

THE SON OF ENCOURAGEMENT

A man called Joseph earned the nickname 'Son of Encouragement' or 'Barnabas' from the Christians in Jerusalem.

His encouragement went further than simply cheering people up —

❖ He was one of the first to sell his possessions to support the believers in Jerusalem.

❖ He was influential in the early church, supporting Paul early in his ministry and on his first missionary journey.

❖ He supported and spurred on his cousin John Mark, despite his mistakes and failures.

❖ "When he arrived and saw the evidence of the grace of God, he was glad and encouraged them all to remain true to the Lord with all their hearts. He was a good man, full of the Holy Spirit and faith, and a great number of people were brought to the Lord" (Acts 11:23–24).

"An act of goodness, the least act of true goodness, is indeed the best proof of the existence of God." **Jacques Maritain**

1 Our work —
2 ▶ is wood, hay or straw (1 Cor 3:12) – it does not
3   have lasting value;
4 ▶ feeds our own ego;
5 ▶ may be the result of guilt or wrongly placed
6   ambition;
7 ▶ maintains the way things have always been;
8 ▶ can become a burden.
9

10 The Lord's work—
11 ▶ is gold, silver and costly stones;
12 ▶ is centred on Christ and his kingdom;
13 ▶ is never a burden. Jesus said, "Take my yoke upon
14   you … . For my yolk is easy and my burden is
15   light" (Matt 11:30).
16

17 WHY WE MAY WANT TO QUIT

18 If serving God were wonderful all the time, then Paul
19 would never have needed to write words of
20 encouragement to spur us on. But the truth is that
21 however committed and called we may feel, there are
22 times when we feel like quitting.
23

24 Ganged up against us are the foes of —

25 Weariness

26 Gal 6:9 and 2 Thes 3:13 remind us not to get tired of
27 doing the right things. But we can through —
28 ▶ Physical tiredness – the slog of doing it. We need
29   to have the right lifestyle that allows us to rest.
30 ▶ Boredom – another kind of tiredness – is made
31   worse by our culture that demands constant new
32   and novel experiences.
33

34 Opposition

35 This can be —
36 ▶ in the spiritual realm – from powers that we
37   cannot see, but which are in opposition to Christ
38   and his kingdom (Col 2:15).
39 ▶ in practical ways – difficult circumstances that
40   life throws up.
41 ▶ within the church – from those who view things
42   differently from us, those who don't respect the
43   truth of God's word, and others.
44

45 Distractions

46 From worthy activities that should not be on our
47 agenda.

"The will to persevere is often the difference between failure and success." **David Sarnoff**

"When the darkness of dismay comes, endure until it is over, because out of it will come that following of Jesus which is an unspeakable joy." **Oswald Chambers**

WORLD MISSION FAMILY THE WORLD OF WORK SPIRITUAL WARFARE

▶ Jesus resisted all distractions and "set his face like 1
a flint" (Is 50:7) for Jerusalem. 2

We may fail to say 'no' because —
▶ We are flattered to be asked
▶ We feel guilty to say 'no'
▶ We see ourself as the best person for the job
▶ We think we won't be liked if we say 'no'

Lack of encouragement

▶ From one another. Our main source of
encouragement should be each other. All
have a responsibility to encourage those
around them in the church, as described in
Col 3:12–17.
▶ From results. In our instant world, at times
we need to see our faithfulness as being the
success we seek.

In the book of Revelation, God has given assurance 21
to successive generations of Christians that these 22
hopes will really happen —
▶ God will prevail, and every knee will bow before 23
Jesus; 24
▶ Evil will be defeated once and for all; 25
▶ We will have a fresh start and a new dwelling 26
place in heaven – a place that knows no sin, no 27
chaos and no heartache, only joy. 28
29

Those who persevere in their faith will share in heaven's 30
riches (Rev 3:5; 21:7). 31
32

OUR RESOURCES 33
The ability to keep going until God's work is completed 34
comes from — 35
▶ Jesus himself – the heart of the message to the 36
Colossians; 37
▶ The power of the Holy Spirit working in us; 38
▶ Faith in God and an ability to see things from his 39
perspective; 40
▶ The support of other people in the body of 41
Christ. 42
43

The key message of Colossians is that Christ and Christ 44
alone is the head of the church. He is the first in 45
everything (Col 1:18). As Christians and members of 46
the church, Christ is our head, our spiritual source of 47

BACKGROUND

THE ART OF SAYING 'NO'

❖ Establish your
priorities before you
are ever asked.

❖ Remember that if
they feel free to ask,
you should feel free
to say 'no'.

❖ Remind yourself
that you have the
right to say 'no'
without feeling
guilty or selfish.

❖ Respond clearly,
firmly and without
long winded
explanation or
excuses.

❖ Stick to it.

❖ Don't hang around.

*"We are sometimes so
occupied with being good
angels that we neglect to be
good men and women."*
Saint Francis de Sales

PRESSING ON
EVANGELISM

FALSE TEACHING
SALVATION
UNLIMITED ENTRY-UNLIMITED
UNLIMITED ENTRY-UNLIMITED

1 life, our guide, counsellor, even our spiritual identity.
2

THE VALUE OF PERSEVERANCE

4 "*We also rejoice in our sufferings, because we know that*
5 *suffering produces perseverance*" (Rom 5:3).
6

7 When we see the potential that suffering has to produce
8 character and hope in our lives, we persevere through it
9 with God's help.
10

11 "*… make every effort to add to your faith …,*
12 *perseverance; and to perseverance, godliness; …*"
13 (2 Pet 1:5–8).
14

15 The Christian life begins with faith but grows through
16 perseverance.
17

18 "*Because you know that the testing of your faith develops*
19 *perseverance*" (James 1:3).
20

21 God's promises encourage us to persevere —
22 ▶ He responds to persistent prayer (Matt 7:7);
23 ▶ He will always be with us (Matt 28:20; John
24   14:18);
25 ▶ He is purposefully working in our lives (Phil 1:6);
26 ▶ He will provide all our needs (Matt 6:33).
27

28 RETURNING TO THE BRIDE

29 All that we do is to be with a sense of expectation. The
30 day is coming when the bridegroom – Jesus – comes to
31 claim his bride – us, the Church (Rev 19:7–9, 21:2).
32

33 In the Jewish culture —
34 ▶ The bridegroom came to the bride's house to
35   fetch her;
36 ▶ It was during the evening;
37 ▶ She did not know the exact time;
38 ▶ Her lamp had to be full and she had to stay
39   awake.
40

41 We are to be working towards being ready for the
42 bridegroom's return to fetch us. The wedding banquet –
43 feast of celebration – will be when Christ returns.
44

45 FINALLY

46 Paul wrote his letter —
47 ▶ to combat errors concerning relationships in the

"*We are called to be the Lord's die-hards, to whom can be committed any kind of trial of endurance, and who can be counted upon to stand firm whatever happens. Surely, fortitude is the sovereign virtue of life; not patience, though we need it too, but fortitude. O God, give me fortitude.*" **Amy Carmichael**

QUESTION ?

To what extent do you see your sevice for Christ as working towards the bridegroom's (Jesus') return?

church; 1

▶ to show that believers have everything they need 2
in Christ; 3

▶ to show that they could tackle today's issues, 4
creating hope for tomorrow; 5

▶ to keep their vision of God clear and 6
untarnished. 7

8

In the same way, we are to be — 9

▶ open to God, because people matter for the sake 10
of Jesus; 11

▶ orthodox in faith and radical in practice; 12

▶ committed to seeing things through to the end. 13

14

The Colossians, like us, needed to take fresh hold on 15
Jesus Christ – on his complete supremacy and utter 16
sufficiency. 17

▶ Paul encourages them and us to work for Christ 18
personally. 19

▶ Paul challenges them and us to have new insights 20
about the glory of Jesus. 21

▶ Paul asks them and us practical questions about 22
our lifestyle in the church, the family, the 23
household and the community. 24

▶ Paul emphasises to them and us the need 25
to put on Christian virtues, values and 26
qualities.

▶ We are called to living out our faith on
the frontiers and margins of society.

▶ Therefore we stop, we look and we listen
as we reflect.

Let's look at Jesus again and at his impact on 33

— 34

▶ those first disciples through his life teaching, 35
ministering, healing, transforming, suffering, 36
dying, rising and ascending; 37

▶ the early church as individuals, groups, crowds, 38
communities and nations; 39

▶ the lives of his followers since, past and present; 40

▶ our own experience. 41

42

Let's listen for God to speak again to us — 43

▶ in our present situation; 44

▶ in the taking and receiving of bread and wine in 45
the sacraments; 46

47

"Anyone who proposes to do good must not expect people to roll stones out of his way, but must accept his lot calmly if they even roll a few more upon it." **Albert Schweitzer**

EXERCISES

Let's stop
▶ rushing so fast,
▶ worrying so often,
▶ doing so much.

1   ❯ in the space, stillness, solitude and quietness of
2   the secular and the sacred;
3   ❯ in meditation and devotion and quietness;
4   ❯ inwardly and outwardly, personally and
5   corporately;
6   ❯ in all the opportunity that life offers today and
7   tomorrow.
8

9 So that, with new-found peace, we can serve —
10   ❯ God our Father and Christ his Son our Lord
11   victorious;
12   ❯ ourselves and others better in the power of the
13   Holy Spirit.
14

15 Therefore put on as God's chosen ones – Christ.
16

17 Look widely – listen attentively – reflect carefully –
18 pray deeply – share generously.
19
20
21
22

"It is a mistake to suppose that God is only, or even chiefly, concerned with religion." **William Temple**

TRAVEL LOG

On my journey to that final frontier Pressing On —

The most interesting thing I saw was ....

....

....

The most surprising thing I saw was ....

....

....

The most important thing I saw was....................................

....

....

Because of my visit, in the future I want to try to ....

....

....

45
46
47